WEEKENDS FOR TWO IN SOUTHERN CALIFORNIA

50 Romantic Getaways

Weekends for Two in Southern California

50 Romantic Getaways

BY BILL GLEESON
PHOTOGRAPHS BY JOHN SWAIN

CHRONICLE BOOKS
SAN FRANCISCO

Library of Congress Cataloging-in-Publication Data
Gleeson, Bill.
    Weekends for two in Southern California :
  50 romantic getaways / by Bill Gleeson and John Swain.
       p.   cm.
     Includes index.
     ISBN 0-8118-0149-7
     1. California, Southern—Guidebooks. I. Title.
  F867.G54   1992
  917.94'90453—dc20   92-13495
                                              CIP

Printed in Hong Kong.

Distributed in Canada by Raincoast Books, 112 East Third
Ave., Vancouver, B.C. V5T 1C8
Editing: Deborah Stone
Book and cover design: Robin Weiss

10 9 8 7 6 5 4 3 2

Chronicle Books
275 Fifth Street
San Francisco, CA 94103

ACKNOWLEDGMENTS

The author and photographer wish to thank the following
for their contributions, inspiration, and support:

Regina Miesch, photographic styling inspiration
Yvonne Gleeson, research assistance
Robert and Ferne Gleeson
Richard and Isabel Gomes
Bill LeBlond
Drew Montgomery
Jerry Hulse
Catalina Cruises

Table of Contents

INTRODUCTION

Memories aren't always misty watercolors.

*I*t seems like only yesterday that the two of us set out for a long-anticipated and much-deserved California romantic weekend. The reservation service had booked a room for us in a "charming, colonial-style B&B," and promised us a weekend to remember. Unfortunately, it was memorable for all the wrong reasons.

The "colonial B&B" turned out to be a contemporary stucco box with two columns propped in front for effect. The guest-room closets held the resident family's flotsam, and the tacky oil paintings adorning the walls were priced to sell.

When we ventured downstairs after settling in, we found the husband-wife hosts were cooking an obnoxious-smelling dinner that sent us quickly back to our room. After a short discussion, we packed our bags, tiptoed out the door, and drove a disappointing two-and-a-half hours back home, without spending the night.

Vowing never to leave another precious weekend to chance, we began an odyssey in search of the north state's most romantic destinations. The result of those travels was the best-selling *Weekends for Two in Northern California, 50 Romantic Getaways.*

ROOMS FOR ROMANCE

Moving on to Southern California, we traveled thousands of miles searching out the region's most sumptuous retreats. From an original list of well over one hundred small hotels and inns, we narrowed the field to fifty using our own set of romantic standards. While there are no definitive rules (after all, what starts our engines may leave you in neutral), there do seem to be certain features that activate the passion buttons in many of us. Our romantic criteria include:

- In-room fireplaces
- In-room tubs or showers built for two (some innkeepers even provide the bubble bath)
- Breakfast in bed or in your room
- Feather beds and cushy comforters
- Canopied four-poster king-sized beds
- Love seats or places to sit together
- Private decks, patios, or balconies with inspirational views
- Outdoor spaces with private places
- Romantic decor, special touches, and accessories

We also selected hotels or inns that, even lacking some of the features above, still exude that sometimes-difficult-to-describe intimate atmosphere.

Finally, we were partial to those establishments where privacy is ensured, where the inn-keeper isn't always underfoot, where interior walls are well insulated, and where child guests are discouraged. While we certainly harbor no prejudice toward children—we have two of our own—many couples are seeking a well-deserved break from the kids. The (sometimes loud) evidence of little people in the room next door or in the hall doesn't exactly contribute to a passionate getaway.

Many inn guidebooks describe, in exhausting detail, lobbies, parlors, and other public areas. We've taken a different approach, choosing to highlight and recommend specific guest rooms that we found conducive to a romantic experience. After all, where are you going to spend most or your time during a romantic getaway?

When you call for a reservation, instead of leaving the choice of rooms to the reservation clerk, don't hesitate to ask about the availability of a specific room, if you have a personal favorite.

CAST YOUR VOTE

Speaking of favorite getaway destinations in Southern California, we'd like to know yours. Cast your vote for the south state's most romantic destination (or let us know if we overlooked one of your special places). Simply complete and return the coupon at the back of this book. We look forward to sharing new romantic weekends for two in future printings.

A WORD ABOUT RATES

While seasoned travelers might still be able to find a room along the highway for less than $50, this guide isn't for bargain hunters. Since romantic getaways are special occasions, we've learned to adjust to the higher tariffs being commanded for that special room. In fact, most of the rooms described in the following pages start at more than $100 per night.

To help you plan your getaway budget, approximate 1993 rates of specific rooms are noted at the end of each description. If you're booking a weekend trip, please note that some of the more popular establishments require a two-night minimum stay. Make sure you inquire about multi-night stays, so you're not surprised when you arrive. (Of course, rates are subject to change without notice.)

Rates (per weekend night for two friendly people) are classified in the following ranges, not including tax:

Moderate: $100–$150
Expensive: $150–$200
Deluxe: Over $200

FINAL NOTES

No payment was accepted from any establishment in exchange for a listing in this book. Inclusion was by invitation only.

Food, wine, and flowers were occasionally added to photos for styling purposes. Some inns provide such amenities; others do not. Please ask at the time you make a reservation whether these items are complimentary or whether they're provided for an extra charge.

The author and the photographer have visited all of the establishments featured in the following pages. We cannot guarantee that these properties will maintain furnishings or standards as they existed on our visit, and we appreciate hearing from readers if their experience is at variance with our description.

The South Central Coast

DAYTIME DIVERSIONS

The region we've designated as the south coast runs from Morro Bay north to Big Sur.

By far the biggest attraction along this part of the coast is Hearst Castle (Hearst San Simeon State Historical Monument). This is an always-busy attraction, so it's best to reserve tickets in advance. (Californians can dial [800] 446-PARK.) For first-time visitors, we recommend Tour One, which takes in an opulent guest house, the magnificent indoor and outdoor pools, and the ground floor of the castle, including the refectory, billiard room, and theater. Mr. Hearst's incredibly romantic boudoir, the Celestial Suite, is on Tour Two.

After castle touring, you might want to visit a few of the dozens of small wineries nearby. Ask your innkeeper for a winery map.

TABLES FOR TWO

Ian's and the Sow's Ear both received high marks from our Cambria innkeepers. The Inn at Morro Bay has an oceanview restaurant serving pasta, meat, and fresh seafood entrées.

AFTER HOURS

Although this part of the coast isn't the nightlife capital of California, there are a few clubs offering entertainment after dark. In Cambria, try Camozzi's Saloon.

POST RANCH INN
Highway 1 (P.O. Box 219), Big Sur, CA 93920
Telephone: toll-free (800) 527-2200

Thirty rooms, each with private bath, working fireplace, Jacuzzi tub, stereo system, massage table, and
refrigerator with complimentary beverages. Continental breakfast included. Basking pool, lap pool,
fitness center, gift shop, and Sierra Mar restaurant
and bar on-site. Handicapped access. Two-night
minimum stay on weekends. Deluxe.

GETTING THERE
Post Ranch Inn is approximately 220 miles (just
over four hours) north of Santa Barbara and about
300 miles (just over six hours) from Los Angeles.
Carmel is 28 miles to the north, and the Monterey
airport is about 35 miles away. The resort is located
on Highway 1 across the road from Ventana.

POST RANCH INN
Big Sur

*I*n assembling this guide, we drew the north/south boundary the scientific way: by folding a California map in half. Big Sur fell just to the south of the fold which was close enough for us.

The newest of our south coast romantic retreats, the upscale Post Ranch Inn opened in mid-1992 after some eight years of development. It carries the distinction of being Big Sur's first major resort in nineteen years.

Set back from Highway 1 and offering unobstructed views of the ocean from a coastal ridge, the inn was designed to blend unobtrusively with the Big Sur environment. (*The New York Times* called it an environmentally correct hotel.)

Rooms for Romance

Like the exterior, guest rooms here exude a rustic coastal elegance. Natural wood and stone are the overriding design elements.

There are four different types of accommodations at Post Ranch Inn. The five Ocean Houses are set into the side of the coastal ridge and topped with sod roofs. Seven Tree

Houses sit on stilts to protect redwood tree roots. Coast Houses—there are ten of these—are cylinder-shaped rooms, and three units are housed in a tri-level Butterfly House. Rates range from around $300 to $450 per night.

Guests are pampered with a variety of luxurious amenities including two pools and a fitness center offering yoga, aerobics, and exercise equipment. For massages, guests needn't go far. Rooms are all equipped with massage tables. Only in Big Sur.

MADONNA INN
100 Madonna Road, San Luis Obispo, CA 93401
Telephone: (805) 543-3000

One-hundred-and-ten rooms, each with private bath; thirteen with fireplaces. Restaurant and shops on-site. Credit cards are not accepted. Handicapped access. Moderate to expensive.

GETTING THERE
The Madonna Inn is approximately a three-and-a-half-hour drive from Los Angeles. In San Luis Obispo, exit Highway 101 at Madonna Road, drive west to inn.

MADONNA INN
San Luis Obispo

A few days after we called the Madonna Inn to ask for advance descriptions of some of their rooms, the mail carrier delivered a bulky package containing more than one hundred postcards, each picturing a different room. Thumbing through them, we immediately understood that the Madonna is beyond description. It's one place you've got to see to believe.

After flustering a succession of architects and designers with visions of two hundred–ton boulders, the owners decided to take things into their own hands. Alex Madonna was behind the controls of the crane when boulders were assembled for the popular Cave Man Room, and his wife, Phyllis, lent her decorating skills, not to mention a bit of tongue-in-cheek humor, to each of the inn's rooms.

Rooms for Romance

This extremely popular motel, the grandfather of California romantic inns, was built in an era when round beds, red velvet wallpaper, and gold chandeliers represented the ultimate in romantic decor.

It was during the 1950s that rancher and freeway and bridge-builder Alex, along with Phyllis, hatched the idea for an inn alongside Highway 101. While written narrative fails to adequately convey the essence of the inn, I'll give it a try.

You'll risk wearing out a pair of shoes in the Austrian Suite (room 160), a room long enough for a bowling alley. Decorated in shades of blue, the room features a pitched ceiling and two balconies, along with king-sized bed.

Although tons and tons of rock have been incorporated into the design throughout the inn, stone is particularly dominant in the Old World Suite (room 192). There's a rock fireplace, rock floors, rock walls, rock shower, and a rock waterfall filling rock basins. Most everything that isn't rock is vivid red in color. The Madonna Suite (room 141) and Cave Man (room 137) also carry the stone theme. "Daisy Mae" (room 138) has the inn's most elaborate rock shower. Rooms 167 through 169 are known as Ron, De, and Vouz. Two have circular beds.

Cherub chandeliers, cherub lamps, cherub art, and cherub wallpaper adorn Cloud Nine (room 161). This bright room, which would have made Liberace beam, features unusual angles, a pitched ceiling, and king-sized bed.

The Madonna Inn is one of those places that probably will leave you hot or cold. Either way, it's a must-see for curious tourists, scores of whom drop in by the busload to take a look. The waterfall in the men's rest room inside the restaurant is so famous that women often sneak in to snap a picture. (Picture postcards are available for the timid.)

A final note. Many traveling romantics will undoubtedly enjoy the rock rooms and some of the inn's other flamboyant accommodations. Keep in mind that these are booked several weeks or months in advance. We couldn't even get in to photograph these popular retreats. However, in our opinion, some rooms seemed better suited to a romantic getaway than others. Unless you've stayed here before and are familiar with the varying decor, our suggestion is to preview your assigned room before registering.

APPLE FARM INN

2015 Monterey Street, San Luis Obispo, CA 93401
Telephone: (805) 544–2040; toll-free (800) 255-
2040

Sixty-seven rooms, each with private bath, television, telephone, and fireplace. Continental breakfast can be delivered to your room at extra cost.
Complimentary coffee and tea delivered to your
room with wake-up call. Restaurant and swimming
pool/spa on-site. Handicapped access. Moderate.

GETTING THERE

From Highway 101 in San Luis Obispo, exit at
Monterey Street and drive east to the inn.

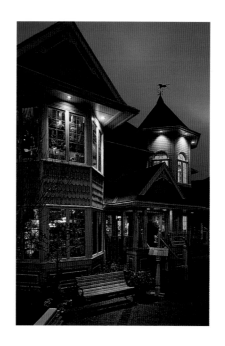

APPLE FARM INN
San Luis Obispo

T he motel-dotted Highway 101 corridor through San Luis Obispo county has never been famous for cozy inns, but innkeepers Bob and Katy Davis are working to change that. The couple, who opened the Apple Farm Coffee Shop here many years ago, are now carving a new niche with the quaint Apple Farm Inn. For traveling twosomes passing through San

Luis Obispo, this is a great place to spend a night, or two. The owners have done well in their efforts to create an intimate atmosphere, despite their location close to the highway.

Guest rooms at Apple Farm borrow from traditional and Victorian themes, characterized by wallpaper, wainscoting, and cozy, turreted seating areas equipped with love seats, wing chairs, and window seats. Each room features a gas fireplace with hearth, and a four-poster or canopied bed of brass or enamel. Mabel Shulz, the Santa Barbara decorator and innkeeper who designed these rooms, is also responsible for the attractive decor at the three Moonstone Beach Drive hideaways in Cambria described in this section.

Rooms for Romance

Two of the rooms, Millhouse A and Millhouse B, are located above Apple Farm Millhouse, a working mill built over San Luis Creek. They both feature king-sized beds, sitting areas, and balconies. Millhouse A overlooks the pool; Millhouse B has a view of the creek and surrounding trees.

Room 300 has an octagonal shape crowned with a skylight set in a turreted ceiling. The king-sized bed is covered with a canopy and the bathroom equipped with an oversized tub. The three aforementioned rooms are priced in the mid $100 range.

THE INN AT MORRO BAY
Morro Bay, CA 93442
Telephone: toll-free (800) 321-9566

Ninety-six rooms, each with private bath; twenty
with gas fireplaces; nine with direct bay views.
Many rooms are equipped with televisions, refrigerators, and balconies. Restaurant and year-round
heated swimming pool on-site; 18-hole golf course
adjacent to the inn. Bicycles are available free to
guests. Moderate to deluxe.

GETTING THERE
Exit Highway 1 at Main Street. Proceed south
through town to Morro Bay State Park entrance.
The resort is on the right, within the park
boundary.

Morro Bay

Situated at water's edge just beyond the shadow of the hulking Morro Rock and within the boundaries of a state park, the Inn at Morro Bay enjoys one of the south state's most romantic locations.

Given its beautiful setting and its location just a half-hour south of Hearst Castle, it's surprising how few people venture to this quiet little corner of the coast. We encountered few folks as we watched for birds (the adjacent bird sanctuary is home to rare species), strolled under tall stands of eucalyptus, and explored the rocky coastal trails. Canoes and bicycles are available to guests.

Rooms for Romance

Twenty of the inn's nearly one hundred rooms are equipped with gas fireplaces. All of these are decorated in the popular country French motif and feature personal-size refrigerators and small balconies. Televisions are hidden inside armoires, and plantation shutters cover the windows.

Room 280 (mid $200 range) is known as the inn's honeymoon room. This oversized chamber has a view of Morro Bay, a king-sized bed, and private balcony. There's a Jacuzzi tub for two in the bathroom.

To avoid disappointment, be sure to request a room with a bay view if that's what you want. Only nine rooms with fireplaces directly overlook the shores of Morro Bay. The best are those offering views of Morro Rock.

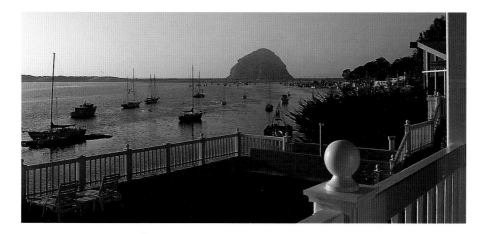

BAYWOOD BED AND BREAKFAST INN
1370 Second Street, Baywood Park, CA 93402
Telephone: (805) 528-8888

Eleven suites and four rooms, each with private bath, microwave, refrigerator, woodburning fireplace, and telephone. Continental breakfast delivered to your room. All rooms and suites have outside entrances. Restaurant on-site. Smoking not permitted. One suite is fitted for guests with disabilities. Two-night minimum on weekends and holidays. Moderate to expensive.

GETTING THERE
From northbound Highway 101, approximately two hundred miles from Los Angeles. Take the Highway 1 exit toward Morro Bay. Exit Highway 1 at South Bay Boulevard (Los Osos/Baywood Park exit) and drive south for two miles to Santa Ysabel. Turn right and drive one mile to Second Street. Turn left; drive two blocks to the inn.

BAYWOOD BED AND BREAKFAST INN

Baywood Park

*I*t's a good thing we knew the address; we might well have mistaken the Baywood Bed and Breakfast Inn for an office complex and driven right on by. Behind this contemporary corporate exterior, however, we discovered more than a dozen enticing thematic rooms and suites.

Whatever your taste, chances are good there's a room here with your name on the door. Theme rooms include the Tex-Mex Suite, decorated with Mexican artifacts; the Avonlea Suite, done in English country style; and the Appalachian, patterned after a mountain cabin with rough-sawn cedar beams, bark-covered tree limb furniture, and a cascading river-rock fireplace.

Rooms for Romance

While all of these accommodations were intriguing, we identified a few that seemed especially suited to traveling romantics. A colonial theme characterizes Williamsburg (low $100 range), a handsome, bay-view room with four-poster canopied bed and brick fireplace. This upper-level room also has a separate dining area.

On the lower level, the Queen Victoria Suite (low $100 range) has a love seat for snuggling in front of the brick fireplace. The separate bedroom holds a brass bed.

Two strategically angled bay windows offer a wide seashore panorama from the upper-level California Beach Room (low $100 range). Tropical plants, seafoam green carpet, and a glass-topped, shell-shaped coffee table complete the scene.

Avonlea and Tex-Mex are both two-bedroom/two-bath suites (mid $100 range) that would work well for two couples traveling together.

SAND PEBBLES INN
6252 Moonstone Beach Drive, Cambria, CA 93428
Telephone: (805) 927-5600

Twenty-three rooms, each with private bath, gas
fireplace, and canopied bed. Handicapped access.
Moderate to expensive.

GETTING THERE
Cambria is six miles south of Hearst Castle. Exit
Highway 1 at Moonstone Beach Drive. Drive west
to the inn.

SAND PEBBLES INN

Cambria

You've scored a couple of tickets to Hearst Castle and you're tempted to drive up the coast and back in a day. After all, there aren't any really romantic places to spend the night in the San Simeon area, right? Wrong! While this might have been true a few years ago, with the recent addition of Sand Pebbles Inn and the other new Moonstone Beach Drive destinations described in this section, couples are lingering in Cambria overnight in greater numbers than ever before.

Located about ten minutes south of Hearst Castle, Sand Pebbles Inn features luxurious custom appointments similar to those found in its sister inn, the Blue Dolphin Inn, just a few doors away. (Both are owned by the same family.)

Rooms for Romance

Guest rooms, many with beautiful ocean views, are lusciously decorated in English country style with bunches of throw pillows, canopied beds with layered ruffles and comforters, decorative lamps, gas fireplaces, and floral wall coverings.

Rooms 117, 118, and 119 (high $100 range) have patios, whirlpool tubs, and canopied beds. On the second floor, rooms 217 and 219 offer beautiful ocean views. Each is furnished with two half-canopied queen-sized beds. Room 218 is a beautiful ocean-view room with a king-sized full-canopied bed. These second floor rooms carry rates in the mid $100 range.

Amenities in each room include a mini refrigerator, books, television, videocassette player, and hair dryer. All rooms have private baths and some are equipped with tubs big enough for two (in a pinch).

A Continental breakfast is served daily, and tea and cookies await guests every afternoon.

The Sand Pebbles and Blue Dolphin inns are reportedly the only two American Automobile Association four-diamond-rated inns between Carmel and San Luis Obispo.

BLUE DOLPHIN INN
6470 Moonstone Beach Drive, Cambria, CA 93428
Telephone: (805) 927-3300

Eighteen rooms, each with private bath.
Continental breakfast and afternoon tea and cookies included. Moderate to expensive.

GETTING THERE
Cambria is six miles south of Hearst Castle. Exit
Highway 1 at Moonstone Beach Drive. Drive west
to the inn.

BLUE DOLPHIN INN
Cambria

*T*he Blue Dolphin Inn (not to be confused with the nearby Blue Whale Inn or its nearly identical sister, the Sand Pebbles Inn) occupies a pretty ocean-view spot just across the road from the Pacific Ocean.

Rooms for Romance

While its architecture, contemporary with a hint of Cape Cod, isn't particularly inspiring, the Blue Dolphin is equipped with lavishly styled rooms that we found to be among the region's most romantic.

English country is the theme carried through the Blue Dolphin's eighteen rooms, each furnished with a gas fireplace, refrigerator, discreetly placed television, and videocassette player. Each room has a private bath; six have tubs that might just be big enough for the two of you. Many of the beds are canopied.

The most popular rooms are 111, 112, and 113, available in the high $100 range. These ground-floor accommodations offer ocean-view patios. If outdoor lounging isn't a must, the front-facing rooms 211, 212, and 214 on the second floor have equally nice ocean views with rates in the mid $100 range.

The inn serves Continental breakfast in the parlor, but guests may request that trays be brought to their rooms. Tea and cookies are served each afternoon.

BLUE WHALE INN
6736 Moonstone Beach Drive, Cambria, CA 93428
Telephone: (805) 927-4647

Six rooms, each with private bath (including hair dryer) and gas fireplace. Complimentary full breakfast served daily in an ocean-view breakfast room. Wine and cheese served every afternoon in the library sitting room. Smoking not permitted indoors. Two-night minimum on weekends and holidays. Moderate to expensive.

GETTING THERE
Cambria is six miles south of Hearst Castle. Exit Highway 1 at Moonstone Beach Drive. Drive west to the inn.

BLUE WHALE INN
Cambria

*F*rom the outside, the Blue Whale Inn doesn't resemble many of the other inns we visited in Southern California. However, neither can it be described as a motel. Its facade is a cross between an inn and an upscale motel—sort of an *inntel*.

Borrowing from the motel model, the Blue Whale's six rooms are all connected, forming a single one-level wing. All similarities stop there, however. Instead of parking in front of the rooms, autos are confined to a common parking area. Rooms, each set back a few feet from the other, are reached via a walkway bordered by a garden area with benches, decorative rock, colorful plantings, and waterfall pond. The inn's redwood exterior is stained gray with white trim.

Rooms for Romance

Rooms at the Blue Whale were designed by Mabel Shults, who also contributed her considerable decorating skills to the Apple Farm Inn, the Inn on Summer Hill, and the nearby Sand Pebbles and Blue Dolphin Inns (all featured in this book).

Ms. Shults encourages innkeeping clients to devote a generous budget to individual room decor, and the owners of the Blue Whale obliged. Guest rooms here are striking and

detailed, characterized by bunches of throw pillows, raised canopied beds with layered ruffles and comforters, decorative lamps (she prefers not to use overhead lighting), plantation shutters, crown molding, floral wallpaper, and pastel colors.

Each room has a distinctive look, and is equipped with a gas fireplace, love seat, small refrigerator, and television (hidden in the armoire). Four rooms have king-sized beds; two have queens. Rates start in the mid $100 range.

THE J. PATRICK HOUSE

2990 Burton Drive, Cambria, CA 93428
Telephone: (805) 927-3812

Eight rooms, each with private bath and fireplace. Continental breakfast (homemade food) and evening wine and cheese served daily. Smoking not permitted on the property. Moderate.

GETTING THERE

Cambria is six miles south of Hearst Castle. Take the Burton Drive exit from Highway 1. Drive east to the inn.

J. PATRICK HOUSE
Cambria

*U*nlike the contemporary seaside lodgings we sampled in Cambria, the J. Patrick House is an old-fashioned, wooded hideaway nestled above the village just to the east of Highway 1.

The inn consists of two buildings: a vintage log home in front, and a rear building in which all but one of the guest rooms are housed. With communal activities confined mostly to the main building, the rear annex affords traveling couples considerable quiet and privacy. Rooms, which do not have televisions or phones, are priced in the low $100 range.

Rooms for Romance

In the Dublin room, a corner retreat on the first floor, a woodburning stove sits before a queen-sized bed. There's also a cozy window seat and a bathroom with shower. At the other end of the annex is Tipperary, a sunny corner with knotty-pine wainscoting and window seat. The bath holds a shower/bath combination.

Limerick, a second-floor corner room, has knotty-pine walls and ceiling, and a brick fireplace. The private bath has a shower/bath combination.

Most often requested by romantics-in-the-know is Clare, the inn's largest room and the only one in the main building. Equipped with a king-sized bed, the room has log walls and a nice view of the pines.

The Central Sierra

DAYTIME DIVERSIONS

Fresno Flats Historical Park on Road 427 in Oakhurst encompasses two historic homes, an old schoolhouse, barn, jail, and wagon collection dating from the gold rush days. It's closed on Mondays.

In the nearby village of Ahwahnee is the Wassama Round House State Historic Park, used by Miwok Indians for religious ceremonies. It's open on weekends.

The Yosemite Mountain Sugar Pine Railroad in Fish Camp transports visitors aboard vintage rail stock on a four-mile ride through forested land. Call (209) 683-7273 for a schedule.

TABLES FOR TWO

Critics from all over the country have heaped rave reviews on Erna's Elderberry House adjacent to Chateau du Sureau in Oakhurst. Chef (and innkeeper) Erna Kubin-Clanin and executive sous chef Christian Mueller offer a magnificent fixed-price dinner of six courses that changes nightly. (Plan on spending more than $100 for two.) We also enjoyed an intimate dinner at the Wawona Hotel's restaurant.

AFTER HOURS

Up here in the hills and mountains, you're on your own after dinner. But isn't that why you came here in the first place?

DUCEY'S ON THE LAKE
P.O. Box 329, Bass Lake, CA 93604
Telephone toll-free nationwide: (800) 350-7463

Twenty rooms and suites, each with private bathroom, fireplace, television, two telephones, deck,
microwave, wet bar, and small refrigerator. Twelve
rooms have tubs for two. Continental breakfast may
be taken in your room. Swimming pool, spa, sauna,
tennis courts, and restaurant on-site. Nonsmoking
rooms available. Two-night minimum stay on weekends; three-night minimum during holiday periods.
Handicapped access. Moderate to deluxe.

GETTING THERE
From Highway 99 in Fresno, take Highway 41
north for approximately forty-five miles. Three
miles past Oakhurst, turn right on Road 222 and
follow for seven miles to Bass Lake. Just past Pines
Village shops, turn right to the resort. The lake is an
hour's drive from Fresno and about two hundred
miles north of Los Angeles.

DUCEY'S ON THE LAKE
Bass Lake

While Bass Lake has long played second fiddle to Yosemite National Park, only fourteen miles away, park-bound romantics are increasingly becoming sidetracked these days by Ducey's on the Lake.

Situated on the lake's edge, with boats tied up just off the back deck, the hotel has the impressive look of those grand wood-and-stone mountain lodges of yesteryear. However, Ducey's, which opened in 1991, has all the modern niceties that are missing from many old mountain hostelries.

Rooms for Romance

Although you can save $10 or so by booking a ground-floor room, we suggest the second-level accommodations where you'll slumber under open pine trusses and cathedral ceilings. Second-floor lake-view suites are available in the mid $100 range, while the units facing the lake are about $30 more. All rooms are split-level in design; each has a king-sized bed, fireplace, terry robe, and private bath; more than half are equipped with Jacuzzi spa tubs for two.

Lakefront spa rooms on the first floor open to a large deck that's open to all Ducey's guests. Second floor spa rooms enjoy a bit more privacy.

Bridalveil and Rudi's Retreat are the lodge's two 750-square-foot luxury honeymoon suites. These carry rates in the mid to upper $200 range. Room rates at Ducey's are considerably less during the value season from November through March.

When you call for reservations, ask about package deals. Around the time of our visit, Ducey's was offering an affordable midweek winter package that included room, dinner for two, and Continental breakfast at a per-couple rate in the mid $100 range.

CHATEAU DU SUREAU
P.O. Box 577, Oakhurst, CA 93644
Telephone (209) 683-6860

Nine rooms, each with private bath and fireplace;
eight have tubs for two. Amenities include feather
beds, goose-down comforters, and compact disc
players. Television and telephone available on
request. Complimentary Continental breakfast can
be delivered to your room. Swimming pool and the
acclaimed Erna's Elderberry House restaurant on-
site. Handicapped access. A 10 percent service
charge will be added to your bill. Deluxe.

GETTING THERE
From Highway 99 in Fresno, drive north on Highway 41 toward Oakhurst, a distance of about forty-
five miles. Just before entering the town of Oakhurst (before you reach the Highway 49 intersec-
tion), turn left on Victoria Lane. Oakhurst is
approximately two-hundred-sixty-five miles from
Los Angeles and an hour's drive from Fresno.

CHATEAU DU SUREAU

Oakhurst

$\mathcal{E}$rna Kubin-Clanin cherishes many vivid childhood memories of the romantic castles in her native Europe. "On every mountainside one could spy a castle; I couldn't help being fascinated by them," she recalled. "I remember staring and wondering what life would have been like inside those walls so long ago."

While she may still dream about life in a medieval castle, since we visited Erna, we can't stop dreaming about hers.

Having traded Austria for the foothills of the Central Sierra, Erna recently created Chateau du Sureau, her own elegant chateau. Take extra care passing through the iron gates of this indulgent estate. Cupid is waiting here with bow poised, and your names are on his arrow.

The chateau is a visual feast. We could gush for hundreds of words, but that would leave less space for the pictures. We'll just tempt you with a few juicy details.

Set on a hilltop among native manzanita and elderberry (*sureau* is French for elderberry), the chateau beckons with intriguing angles, rooflines, and windows, a style common to Old World estates, where the addition of multiple generations of family brought new rooms and wings.

Rooms for Romance

Thyme, the least expensive (mid $200 range) of the nine rooms, is actually the largest. Located on the ground floor, the room has a second entry via a courtyard with fish pond. The king-sized bed, arched windows, and French doors are wrapped in subtle Provencal fabrics of olive green.

The ultraromantic Lavender Room (low $300 range), set high in the corner overlooking the pool, offers guests the most castlelike experience. The slate turret is visible from an arched window adjacent the king-sized sleigh bed. The chateau's coat-of-arms is embedded in a wall just outside another window. The fireplace is made of limestone, and the Parisian wrought-iron balcony offers a dramatic view.

Our home for a very special night, the Elderberry Room (mid $300 range), held a king-sized canopy bed dressed in sumptuous shades of blue-and-white Provencal fabric. The ceiling was high and sloped, with hand-carved, whitewashed beams. Our step-up tub for two looked out over terra-cotta rooftops and was positioned nicely for sunset soaking.

In the chateau's grand public areas there are myriad surprises: a music tower with French grand piano, a tiny chapel, and splendid European antiques. We'll leave the other discoveries to you.

Santa Barbara and the Santa Ynez Valley

DAYTIME DIVERSIONS

In Santa Barbara, State Street ends on Stearns Wharf. Many restaurants are nearby. There are at least a half-dozen beaches along this part of the city's coast, and a bike path skirts much of the seashore. The zoo is located at Cabrillo Boulevard at East Beach.

Santa Barbara's vintage Spanish-style downtown offers great shopping, theaters, and dining. The Santa Barbara Mission, considered the queen of the California missions, is on upper Laguna Street (near Mission Street).

Santa Ynez Valley is dotted with more than two dozen small wineries, many of which are within easy reach of Solvang, Ballard, and Los Olivos. Your inn will likely have copies of a winery map.

There are numerous art galleries worth a look in tiny Los Olivos. The immensely popular Danish-style village of Solvang on Highway 246 is also worth a tour, especially for first-time visitors. Nearby Lake Cachuma offers boating and horseback riding.

TABLES FOR TWO

Pop star and Santa Ynez Valley resident Michael Jackson booked the entire restaurant at Los Olivos Grand Hotel during Elizabeth Taylor's 1991 wedding celebrations. Mattei's Tavern in Los Olivos is another popular dining spot.

In Santa Barbara, the downtown area is home to a changing list of restaurants too numerous to mention. Ask your innkeeper for a current recommendation.

AFTER HOURS

The lounge at Santa Barbara's El Encanto offers a dazzling display of city lights. In Santa Ynez Valley, nighttime diversions include Solvang's summer Theaterfest under the stars (June through September) and Mattei's Tavern for an after-dinner refreshment.

THE UPHAM HOTEL & GARDEN COTTAGES

1404 De la Vina Street, Santa Barbara, CA 93101

Telephone: (805) 962-0058

Forty-nine rooms, each with private bath, television, and telephone; eight rooms with fireplaces. Complimentary Continental breakfast buffet, afternoon wine and cheese, and evening coffee and cookies served daily. Privately owned restaurant on-site. Two-night minimum for many weekends and holiday periods. Handicapped access. Moderate to deluxe.

GETTING THERE

From northbound Highway 101 in Santa Barbara, exit at Arrellaga Street, north to De la Vina Street. Turn right to hotel. From southbound Highway 101, exit north on Mission Street; turn right on De la Vina Street to hotel.

THE UPHAM HOTEL &
GARDEN COTTAGES
Santa Barbara

*H*aving outlived the region's many original resort hotels from the 1800s, the Upham has taken title as Southern California's oldest continuously operating hostelry. The venerable Italianate inn has graced this sunny Santa Barbara corner for well over a century.

The Upham complex consists of the main building, an adjacent two-story structure with a dozen rooms, smaller cottage buildings, and a carriage house situated on a well-groomed acre of lawn dotted with white Adirondack lawn furniture.

Rooms for Romance

For a romantic getaway, the cottages and carriage house contained our favorite rooms. The garden cottages have queen-sized beds (some are four-posters) and private patios and/or small porches. Some have fireplaces. Room 42 in the Lotus Cottage (low $100 range) is privately situated behind a gate, so the French doors could be left open on a sunny day. This cozy little room has an iron queen-sized bed and a ceiling fan. The Rose Cottage, room 30, with a four-poster, queen-sized bed, fireplace, and private porch (mid $100 range), is another nice romantic retreat.

The five recently refurbished carriage house rooms feature Ralph Lauren decor; all have four-poster beds.

In the main building, the Master Suite (high $200 range) offers guests a private yard with hammock and lawn furniture, separate living room with fireplace and refrigerator, and a bedroom with king-sized brass bed. There's also a spa tub for two and a shower with double heads.

EL ENCANTO HOTEL AND GARDEN VILLAS
1900 Lasuen Road, Santa Barbara, CA 93103
Telephone: (805) 687-5000

One hundred rooms, each with private bathroom, television, and telephone; thirty-nine with fireplaces. Amenities include bathrobes, hair dryers, and refrigerators. Swimming pool and highly rated restaurant on-site. Moderate to deluxe.

GETTING THERE
From Highway 101, exit at Mission Street and follow signs to Mission Santa Barbara. Veer right at fork onto Alameda Padre Serra for one-half mile. Veer left at next fork onto Lasuen. El Encanto Hotel is on the right.

EL ENCANTO HOTEL
AND GARDEN VILLAS

Santa Barbara

*I*ntimate personal details of a romantic getaway may smolder in the memory for years, but the images of a particular destination can fade with time. Unless the place is as special as El Encanto.

One of our favorite destinations, El Encanto (Spanish for *enchantment*) is quintessential Southern California, with sweeping views of the distant ocean, swaying palms, quaint cottages, and tropical grounds. Its privacy—most cottages are secluded along narrow pathways behind mature trees and shrubbery—has lured many famous couples over the years. We've sampled the room favored by Dudley Moore and Susan Anton (not even El Encanto could hold that relationship together), visited the remote cottage where Tom Selleck and his bride honeymooned, and toured Jane Seymour's oft-requested digs.

Accommodations at El Encanto are varied. Sharing the ten-acre hillside are cozy, board-and-batten cottages dating from the 1930s, whitewashed adobe villas, and condominium-style buildings constructed during the 1970s. Most rooms feature French country decor.

Rooms for Romance

The Wishing Well Cottage (room 322) has a private porch, king-sized bed, and fireplace, as well as a spectacular view over the city to the Channel Islands. And yes, there's a wishing well, too. This room is offered in the high $200 range.

In the low $200 range is room 301, a secluded, free-standing villa situated near the pool. Done in a tasteful green color scheme, it's equipped with a king-sized bed and fireplace, as well as sitting area.

If you're wondering why El Encanto has been designated a historic landmark, try cottage 237, a cozy older bungalow (low $100 range) with queen-sized bed, fireplace, and kitchenette. From personal experience, we can also highly recommend cottage 316 (private hillside setting with French doors), villa 306 (glass porch, kitchenette, adobe fireplace, and glorious view), and villa 329, actually a free-standing cottage suite with spacious porch surrounded by lush gardens

During the daytime, guests often chart a course for Santa Barbara's charming downtown, tour the nearby mission, or lounge at the hotel pool. Evenings at El Encanto are quiet hours, the waters of the trellis-fringed pond rippled only by resident goldfish. Couples stroll hand-in-hand along the winding brick pathways or cuddle in hushed conversation in the yellow swinging love seats that dot the grounds. Not too long after nightfall, the walkways empty as guests retreat to their cottages.

SAN YSIDRO RANCH
900 San Ysidro Lane, Montecito, CA 93108
Telephone: (805) 969-5046

Forty-three cottages, rooms, and suites; each with fireplace, king-sized bed, and porch or deck; thirteen with spas. Amenities include bathrobes and refrigerators. Pool and restaurant/lounge on-site. Horses available. Handicapped access. Expensive to deluxe.

GETTING THERE
From Highway 101 south of Santa-Barbara, exit at San Ysidro Road; drive northeast (away from ocean) to San Ysidro Lane. Turn right to ranch.

SAN YSIDRO RANCH
Santa Barbara

Wandering the grounds of San Ysidro Ranch, we half expected to discover a camera crew on the heels of Robin Leach. This is definitely *the* place where the rich and famous unwind in Santa Barbara. Just take a look at the brochure. "Our ranch," it states, "benevolently tends the well and not-so-needy."

The ranch's lengthy register of not-so-needy guests has included the John F. Kennedys, who honeymooned here (in Upper Hill), and Laurence Olivier and Vivien Leigh, who long ago recited their marriage vows on the grounds. More recently, Mick Jagger and Jerry Hall retreated to the ranch's remote Forest Cottage, and Dennis Quaid and Meg Ryan chose Weingand North for one of their getaways from Hollywood. Mogul Jon Peters loved the resort so much that he almost bought it a few years back.

Because each cottage, room, and suite has a personality all its own, there's no pat description for the ranch. Having served as a guest retreat for the better part of a century, the complex is an attractive mix of old and new. All accommodations here are luxurious. Where else can you expect to find your name engraved on a little sign outside your door?

Rooms for Romance

Rooms at San Ysidro Ranch start in the mid to high $100 range. The Forest Cottage (mid $400 range) is the ranch's most secluded spot, presiding over a couple of beautiful acres. This rustic cottage has a living room and bedroom, a kitchenette, and private deck with

built-in spa. Lilac One and Lilac Two have private spas overlooking the woods.

Other particularly romantic quarters include Geranium Cottage (low $400 range) and rooms 1 and 10 in the Canyons building (around $200). Surprisingly enough, East Upper Hill, where the Kennedys honeymooned, is among the ranch's least expensive rooms, offered in the mid to high $100 range.

HARBOUR CARRIAGE HOUSE
420 West Montecito Street,
Santa Barbara, CA 93101
Telephone: (805) 962–8447; or
toll-free (800) 594-4633

Nine rooms, each with private bath, six with fireplaces, two with tubs for two. Full breakfast served
daily in the solarium. Refreshments served every
evening. Amenities include chocolates, extra thick
towels and potpourri. Television in parlor area only;
phones available on request. Smoking permitted
outside only. Two-night minimum stay required on
weekends and during holiday periods. Handicapped
access. Moderate to expensive.

GETTING THERE
From northbound Highway 101, exit at Cabrillo
Boulevard/Beach. Turn left on Cabrillo and drive for
three miles; right on Castillo for two blocks; left on
West Montecito Street for half a block to inn. From
southbound Highway 101, exit at Castillo Street.
Turn right on Castillo and drive one block; turn
right on West Montecito Street for half a block.

HARBOUR CARRIAGE HOUSE
Santa Barbara

With more than two dozen inns open for business, Santa Barbara might well be the bed-and-breakfast capital of Southern California. To help minimize the element of chance in choosing just the right inn or small hotel, we did some romantic research to narrow the field. Harbour Carriage House is among the standouts.

What is now a nine-room inn started as a single-family home nearly a century ago. The carriage house, whose five second-floor rooms impressed us most, was added not long ago as part of the inn conversion. Guests park in the carport under the carriage house rooms.

Rooms for Romance

Magnolia Blossom and Forget-Me-Not, our two favorite guest rooms (upper $100 range), were equipped with three features virtually guaranteed to set a romantic mood: a king-sized bed, fireplace, and spa tub for two. Forget-Me-Not has a canopied bed and private balcony.

Also in the carriage house is Sweet Alyssum (low $100 range), where French doors open to a private balcony. Next door is French Lilac (low $100 range), whose features include a fireplace, private balcony, and queen-sized antique pine bed. Crimson Rose is similarly equipped with queen-size antique iron bed, fireplace, and private balcony.

Under the garret of the main house's second floor is Lily of the Valley, which faces the lush gardens of two historic homes next door. This room (mid $100 range) has an open-beamed ceiling, king-sized bed, and a day bed.

Harbour Carriage House can be a bit hard to find. Accessed from a busy road via a narrow drive adjacent to the main house, the inn isn't marked by obvious signage. Parking is at the rear of the property at the end of the driveway.

TIFFANY INN
1323 De la Vina Street, Santa Barbara, CA 93101
Telephone: (805) 963-2283

Seven rooms, five with private baths; five with fireplaces, two with tubs for two. A full breakfast is
served on the veranda or in the dining room. Only
guests staying in the suites may bring breakfast to
their rooms. Complimentary refreshments served
every afternoon and evening. This is a nonsmoking
inn. Two-night minimum stay required on weekends
and during holiday periods. Moderate to expensive.

GETTING THERE
From northbound Highway 101, exit at Arrellaga.
Driving east on Arrellaga, turn right on De la Vina
Street. Drive three blocks to the inn. From southbound Highway 101, exit at Mission and proceed
east to De la Vina. Turn right and drive seven
blocks to the inn.

TIFFANY INN
Santa Barbara

*U*nlike other bed-and-breakfast inns that take their names from owners past and present, the Tiffany Inn wasn't named after current proprietors Larry and Carol MacDonald. Tiffany is the spunky black cocker spaniel that greets visitors to this stately older Santa Barbara residence.

While it may not be located in one of Santa Barbara's most affluent neighborhoods, the Tiffany Inn emerged on our list as one of the city's most romantic bed-and-breakfast retreats.

Rooms for Romance

The inn's seven guest rooms are spread among all three levels of the green shingled home. The five that offer private baths (Rose Garden and Nichole share a bathroom) carry rates ranging from the low to upper $100 range. Rooms are not equipped with phones or televisions.

On the main floor facing the garden is the Honeymoon Suite, with private entrance, woodburning fireplace, and sunken tub for two. Guests in this suite are treated to breakfast in bed.

The spacious Penthouse Suite occupies the entire third level, with fireplace, private ocean-view balcony, separate sitting area, and a tub for two. The two suites are the inn's most expensive accommodations.

Sommerset, on the second floor, looks out over mature trees in the front yard. The room is furnished with an antique walnut bed with matching dresser and a beautiful fireplace. The bathroom is equipped with a vintage clawfoot tub and pull-chain toilet.

Also on the second floor is Victoria's, illuminated by tall French windows that open onto the garden area. A fireplace with mirrored mantle sits before the bed and a ceiling fan turns overhead.

The Melrose, the least expensive room (with private bath), is a garden-view retreat with brass bed, corner fireplace, ceiling fan, and a bathroom with pedestal sink.

When guests venture out of their rooms, they often head for the backyard deck, where green wicker furniture sits under a spring-blooming jacaranda tree.

THE CHESHIRE CAT
36 West Valerio Street, Santa Barbara, CA 93101
Telephone: (805) 569-1610

Fifteen rooms, each with private bath and telephone; some with television. Complimentary
breakfast served in the dining room or on the patio.
Complimentary wine served Saturday evening.
Amenities include chocolates, liqueurs, and fresh
flowers. Bicycles available free to guests. No smoking indoors. Two-night minimum stay on weekends.
Moderate to expensive.

GETTING THERE
From Highway 101, take the Mission Street exit
(west) and drive to State Street. Turn right on State
and drive three blocks. Turn right on Valerio to inn.

THE CHESHIRE CAT
Santa Barbara

The two elegant old homes that comprise the Cheshire Cat sit behind a white picket fence on a quiet, palm-lined residential street a short walk from Santa Barbara's bustling shopping district.

The houses are joined by a brick patio courtyard, where, during our visit, several couples enjoyed breakfast in the warm Santa Barbara sun. A spa has been placed discreetly in the pretty white gazebo at the rear of the property.

One of the city's more recent bed-and-breakfast conversions (it opened in 1985), the Cheshire Cat is among a select few older properties that measured up to many of our romantic standards. Each of the fifteen refurbished rooms has its own bath, and four offer tubs for two. Three rooms have fireplaces, and all feature Laura Ashley decor with brass and iron beds.

Rooms for Romance

As if the inn's name didn't give it away, the theme here is Alice in Wonderland, and rooms carry names and decorating touches inspired by the story. The sunny Queen of

Hearts room (high $100 range) is decorated in bright pastels and has wicker furniture. A Jacuzzi tub for two sits under a bay window with wooden shutters.

The split-level Caterpillar (mid to upper $100 range) features two bay window seats in the lower sitting area. The queen-sized bed sits a couple of steps up. A private balcony overlooks the rear garden and gazebo area.

Duchess (mid $100 range) holds the house's original clawfoot tub as well as English antiques. The room is done in a pink floral motif. The Cheshire Cat room (mid to upper $100 range) is a high-ceilinged suite with Jacuzzi tub and built-in television and VCR.

INN ON SUMMER HILL
2520 Lillie Avenue, Summerland, CA 93067
Telephone: toll-free (800) 845-5566

Sixteen rooms, each with private bath, gas fireplace,
comforter, single-person Jacuzzi tub, balcony or
patio, two telephones, television, and videocassette
player. Full breakfast included. Complimentary
afternoon wine and cheese and evening dessert
served daily. Amenities include bathrobes and hair
dryers. Outdoor spa on-site. This is a nonsmoking
inn. Two-night stay required during weekends and
holiday periods. One room is specially designed for
handicapped access. Expensive to deluxe; weekday
rates are significantly lower.

GETTING THERE
From Highway 101, take Summerland exit. Follow
frontage road (along east side of highway) north a
short distance to the inn.

INN ON SUMMER HILL
Summerland

Guests at the Inn on Summer Hill face a pleasant, albeit difficult choice, particularly on a sunny Southern California afternoon. Although the beach beckons from your balcony, the guest rooms here are so comfortable you may find yourselves opting for a cushy sofa.

Rooms for Romance

With knotty pine ceilings, canopied beds draped with yards of tasteful fabric, goose-down comforters, rich moldings, corner fireplaces, and sunny balconies, these rooms, designed by owner and decorator Mabel Shults, will remind you of those luscious retreats pictured in decorating magazines—a dream bedroom come true.

For example, in room 5 downstairs, a delightful combination of stripe and floral drapes cascade down the four posts of a king-sized bed. Red-and-white gingham bows are tied to each post. The patterns are carried over to the double dust ruffle, pillow shams, tablecloth, and lamp shades.

The stripe and floral combination is featured in other rooms including room 12, done in hues of blue, mauve, and white. Room 4 (green with touches of red) has hardwood floors, a fainting couch, and king-sized bed with an ornate, German antique headboard carved with the inscription, *Gute Nacht*. Each room holds an antique chest. King and queen rooms carry rates in the upper $100 range. One suite is available in the mid $200 range.

Guests who would like to take breakfast in the privacy of their room will awake to find a tray filled with a hot breakfast entree, homemade breads, cereal, fresh fruit, juice, and muffins outside their door. (There is a small fee for this service.) A similar spread is served at a communal table in the dining room.

Reminiscent of a New England country estate, the Inn on Summer Hill sits on a hillside in the oceanside village of Summerland, just ten minutes south of Santa Barbara. Guests may rent bicycles or stroll to the beach. Be sure to take a drive through the exclusive neighborhoods of adjacent Montecito to glimpse the rambling estates of the rich and famous.

A note to those looking for a retreat as far from the madding crowd as possible: Be aware that the Inn on Summer Hill sits fairly close to Highway 101. Although the highway can be seen from the upstairs guest rooms (bushes block the road view from the main level), traffic noise does not present a problem, thanks to soundproofing.

LOS OLIVOS GRAND HOTEL
2860 Grand Avenue (P.O. Box 526),
Los Olivos, CA 93441
Telephone: (805) 688-7788;
toll-free (800) 446-2455

Twenty-one rooms, each with private bath, gas fireplace, wet bar/refrigerator, television, telephone,
and complimentary bottle of local wine; five with
Jacuzzi tubs for two. Continental breakfast and
morning paper delivered to room. Restaurant,
swimming pool, and spa on-site. Two rooms have
handicapped access. Expensive to deluxe.

GETTING THERE
From southbound Highway 101 south of Los Ala-
mos, take the Highway 154 exit and drive two miles
to the hotel on Grand Avenue. From northbound
Highway 101 just past Santa Barbara, take the
Highway 154 exit and drive twenty-eight miles to
the hotel on Grand Avenue. Los Olivos is approximately one-hundred-forty miles north of Los Angeles and approximately thirty miles south of Santa
Maria.

LOS OLIVOS GRAND HOTEL
Los Olivos

A spur-of-the-moment decision to take the scenic route to Santa Barbara via the pretty Santa Ynez Valley introduced us to the tiny burg of Los Olivos and its Grand Hotel.

While its charming turret and gables suggest a feeling of yesteryear, you won't confuse the hotel with the many pre-1900 buildings that dot the town's main street. The Grand is very much a contemporary hotel offering romantic luxuries unknown during Los Olivos' early days.

If the hotel appears smaller than its twenty-one rooms, that is because about half the accommodations, along with the swimming pool and spa, are across the street in a separate building. The hotel's highly rated restaurant, public areas, and registration desk are on the first floor of the main wing. There are ten guest rooms upstairs.

Often visited by celebrities seeking rest and relaxation (Joan Collins is among those who have slept here), the Grand Hotel's restaurant, Remington's, was the site of an elaborate 1991 wedding celebration hosted for Elizabeth Taylor by her friend, Michael Jackson, whose sprawling ranch is just down the road. The singer booked the entire hotel for the wedding party.

Rooms for Romance

Each of the hotel's rooms is equipped with tiled, gas fireplace, remote-controlled television, telephone, wet bar/refrigerator, and down comforter. Western or French impressionist artworks adorn the walls, and a complimentary bottle of local wine is placed in each room. Continental breakfast is served in your room.

Weekend rates (Sunday through Thursday rates are lower) for a standard room with king-sized bed are in the low $200 range. A larger Master King room runs approximately $200. Five rooms (low $100 range) have two queen-sized beds.

Five rooms with king-sized beds and Jacuzzi tubs for two are offered in the mid $200 range.

THE ALISAL
1054 Alisal Road, Solvang, CA 93463
Telephone: (805) 688-6411

Seventy-three rooms, each with private bath and woodburning fireplace. Full breakfast and dinner included in daily rates. Jackets required for men at dinner. No televisions or telephones in rooms; these are located in public areas throughout the resort. Restaurant, pool, spa, golf course, and tennis courts on-site. Two-night minimum stay required; three-and-four-night minimum stay required during some holiday weekend periods. A 12 percent service charge is added to room rate at check out. Handicapped access. Deluxe.

GETTING THERE
From Highway 101, take the Solvang exit at Buellton. Follow signs to Solvang. Turn right at Alisal Road and follow past golf course to resort. Solvang is approximately one-hundred-thirty-five miles north of Los Angeles.

THE ALISAL
Solvang

The Alisal is a ten-thousand-acre guest ranch spread among the oaks on rolling hills just outside Solvang. Extremely popular during the summer with vacationing families, The Alisal is a destination resort offering just about any conceivable activity.

These activities include golf on a highly rated 18-hole PGA course, guided horseback rides, tennis on seven courts, and swimming. There's even a private ninety-acre lake offering fishing, as well as (sail, motor, and pedal) boat and windsurfing rentals. Wine tastings featuring regional vintages are held regularly.

Rooms for Romance

While the resort is crowded with families and children during much of the summer, the off-season is a great time for couples to visit.

The quaint ranch-style cottages are furnished simply and comfortably, the assumption being that you'll be spending most of your time outdoors. The Alisal does offer studios; however, these are furnished with twin beds. For traveling romantics, we recommend an Executive Studio with king-sized bed, outside patio, and woodburning fireplace. Daily rates, *including breakfast and dinner*, are in the mid $200 range. Golf, tennis, boat rental, and horseback riding fees are extra.

THE INN AT PETERSEN VILLAGE

1576 Mission Drive, Solvang, CA 93463
Telephone: (805) 688-3121; toll-free from within
California (800) 321-8985

Forty rooms, each with private bath, television, and
telephone; two rooms with fireplaces. Complimentary European-style buffet breakfast (ham, cheeses,
cereals, pastries, and beverage) served each morning
in the courtyard lounge. Complimentary wine hour
each evening with piano entertainment. Complimentary coffee and tea room service. Moderate to
expensive.

GETTING THERE

From Highway 101, take the Solvang exit at Buellton. Follow signs to Solvang. The inn is on Mission
Drive at the heart of town. Solvang is approximately one-hundred-thirty-five miles north of Los
Angeles.

THE INN AT
PETERSEN VILLAGE
Solvang

While many Solvang visitors are satisfied with a morning or afternoon shopping encounter, we continually meet people who admit to a longtime romantic fascination with this Danish-style village. For these folks, a visit to Solvang won't be complete without an overnight stay in the half-timbered Inn at Petersen Village.

Located at the center of town, the family-operated inn is the cornerstone of Petersen Village, which includes a Danish bakery and coffee shop, two restaurants, and more than twenty specialty shops.

After negotiating the village's crowded streets, a step inside the quiet, softly lit inn presents a refreshing change. Danish antiques and black-vested bellboys create a charming Scandinavian atmosphere.

Rooms for Romance

The guest rooms feature exposed beams and chintz fabrics. Most are furnished with raised and canopied king- and queen-sized beds (with stepping stools), and antiques. Televisions are hidden inside armoires.

Lest the sight of American autos on Mission Drive remind you that you're still in Southern California, we recommend, to prolong your Danish experience, the second-floor rooms facing the quaint interior courtyard. These carry rates in the mid $100 range.

Of particular note is the three-level suite that occupies the ornate, half-timbered tower facing the driveway. The Tower Suite (low $200 range) holds two bathrooms, dual spa tub, fireplace, wet bar, king-sized, four-poster bed, two televisions, and two phones.

BALLARD INN
2436 Baseline, Ballard, CA 93463
Telephone: (805) 688-7770

Fifteen themed rooms with soundproof walls, each
with private bath (three of the rooms are contained
in an adjacent annex); seven rooms have woodburning fireplaces. Amenities include wine soap, wine
hand lotion, champagne shampoo, and welcome
snack basket. Television is located in public room.
No phones. Full breakfast and afternoon refreshments served daily. Regional wines available for pur-
chase. Smoking permitted only on the outdoor
porch. A 10 percent service charge will be added to
bill at check out. One room has handicapped
access. Expensive to deluxe.

GETTING THERE
From northbound Highway 101, exit at Route 246
(Buellton) and drive east through Solvang. Turn left
on Alamo Pintado Road and follow to Ballard. Turn
right on Baseline to inn. From southbound Highway 101, exit at Route 154 and follow to Los Olivos. Turn right on Alamo Pintado Road and follow
to Ballard. Turn left on Baseline to inn.

BALLARD INN
Ballard

*I*f you're among those who enjoy the Victorian styling of older bed-and-breakfast inns but appreciate the modern niceties of a small luxury hotel, have we got a destination for you. In our travels throughout the southland, we've yet to discover an inn that more romantically melds the best of both eras than the Ballard Inn.

One of Southern California's best-kept secrets, the Ballard is a picture postcard country inn. A covered porch runs the length of the inn, under clapboard gables and turrets, with a little balcony tucked here and an arched window there. Every embellishment is here, including daisies and a white picket fence.

Step inside and you won't be disappointed. The four attractive common rooms on the main floor set the stage for the upstairs guest chambers, each designed to commemorate the people, places, and events that have shaped the Santa Ynez Valley. Catherine Kaufman designed the rooms.

Rooms for Romance

The Mountain Room, arguably the nicest in the house (high $100 range), offers stunning views of the mountains through windows on three sides and from a private balcony. The room is furnished with a king-sized bed and warmed by a working fireplace.

One of the most unusual guest retreats you'll find anywhere in Southern California is the Davy Brown Room (upper $100 range) designed in honor of a former Ballard townsman who rode with the Texas Rangers and trapped with Kit Carson. Three of the room's walls are beamed and mortared to resemble a log cabin. There's a rock fireplace, early American antiques; and, at the time of our visit, a coonskin cap hung from a chair. Old snowshoes and a stuffed pheasant enhanced the spirit of the room.

Other historic themes are celebrated in the Western Room where an old pair of cowboy chaps adorn the wall and steer horns are mounted over the bed. Jarado's Room features a Native American motif. Rates are in the mid $100 range.

Morning sun floods the turret sitting area of the Vineyard Room. A willow bed and willow furniture sit on a blond hardwood floor. Cynthia's Room, a tribute to the so-called first lady of Ballard, features a fireplace and a bed covered with a double wedding ring quilt.

Another attraction of the Ballard Inn is the food. Guests are treated to a full breakfast, cooked to order and served in the antique-filled dining room. The granola and baked goods are made on the premises. Afternoon wine, tea, and appetizers are also served.

Before checking out, be sure to sign your wine cork and throw it in the basket downstairs for luck. Maybe you'll be lucky enough to return.

Catalina Island

GETTING TO CATALINA
Most people travel to Avalon by boat, and there are multiple carriers. Plan on spending $30 or more for a round-trip ticket. Catalina Cruises, with the largest fleet, sails large vessels to Avalon from Long Beach and San Pedro. Catalina Channel Express offers the fastest ships to the island (Long Beach to Avalon in about an hour). Both offer tickets through Ticketron. Catalina Passenger Service operates a large catamaran out of Newport Beach, while Catalina Pacifica plies the ocean between San Diego and Catalina. Plane and helicopter service is also available.

For current phone numbers and transportation details, request an island guide from the Catalina Island Chamber of Commerce/Visitors Bureau at (310) 510-1520.

DAYTIME DIVERSIONS
There are plenty of shops to explore in Avalon village. The harbor beach is a popular destination on sunny days. Many folks walk down early and lay claim to the best spots on the sand with their beach towels, then head back to bed for a few extra winks.

If you'd like to see more of Catalina, rent a golf cart (there's a rental shop near the boat terminal) and explore the inland region of the island on your own, or buy a ticket for an open-air tram tour. Other tours include a glass-bottom boat ride, coastal cruise to Seal Rocks, flying fish boat tour (at night), and a tour of the famous Avalon casino. You can also rent bicycles in Avalon or arrange a horseback ride.

The visitor information center on Crescent Avenue across from the foot of the green Pleasure Pier has brochures to help plan your island activities.

TABLES FOR TWO
Two dinner cruises are offered by the Santa Catalina Island Company. The four-hour Twilight Dining at Two Harbors dinner includes a fourteen-mile sightseeing cruise along the Catalina coast to Two Harbors. A sunset buffet is served aboard a paddle boat during a two-hour cruise. Both are offered from mid-June through mid-September and are priced in the $30 range.

For those who prefer dining on dry land, our Catalina innkeepers recommended Pirrones (in the Hotel Vista del Mar building), The Channel House (oceanfront), Portofino Restaurant (at Hotel Villa Portofino), and Cafe Prego (near the boat pier).

AFTER HOURS
Avalon is one of California's most romantic (and, according to the locals, among the safest) villages. A stroll down the lamp-lit seaside promenade to the sparkling casino has the makings of one of California's best memories. Many of the village shops are open late, and there are a number of quiet and not-so-quiet clubs to choose from.

INN ON MT. ADA
P.O. Box 2560, Avalon, CA 90704
Telephone: (310) 510-2030

Six rooms and suites, each with private bath (room
5 has a three-quarter bath); four rooms with fireplaces. Full dinner and breakfast for two is included
in tariff. Complimentary food and drinks and gas-
powered golf cart also provided. Television available
on request. No smoking in rooms. Deluxe.

GETTING THERE
When you reach the island boat terminal, call the
inn to request taxi service. The ride is free.

INN ON MT. ADA

Avalon

*H*aving spent the better part of a year searching out Southern California's most romantic getaways, we had been overwhelmed with inspiring views and sensual surroundings by the time we reached Long Beach Harbor. Cruising to Catalina on the last leg of our sojourn, we wondered whether we'd already seen the best of the bunch. Then we spied the Inn on Mt. Ada sparkling like a jewel on the hillside. As we headed up the hill aboard an island taxi, we had the distinct feeling the best had been saved for last.

We were right. Savoring what is probably California's most inspiring view, from our bed, no less, we decided life couldn't get much better.

Converted to an inn only a few years ago, this opulent, Georgian-style mansion was built by the late chewing-gum mogul and Chicago Cubs–owner William Wrigley, Jr. for his wife, named—you guessed it—Ada. (Wrigley didn't just own the home; he bought the whole island, reportedly sight unseen.) After the Wrigley years, the home sat abandoned for some time until innkeepers Susie Griffin and Marlene McAdam stepped in and restored it to its former glory.

Rooms for Romance

Mr. Wrigley's private bedroom and living room now comprise the Grand Suite, which carries a weekend and summer rate in the high $500 range. (All room rates include dinner, breakfast, deli-style lunch, and private use of a golf cart.) This may be among the south state's most expensive guest rooms, but it's also one of the most magnificent. Included are an opulently furnished sitting area, queen-sized canopied bed in the sleeping chamber, private bath, marble fireplace, and private bay-view terrace furnished with lounge chairs.

Mrs. Wrigley had her own adjacent private bedroom suite and bath on the second floor. Now known as the Second Suite (around $500), it features a tile-trimmed fireplace, sitting area with fainting couch, and a romantically draped, four-poster queen-sized bed.

The inn's best view (in our opinion) is offered from room 3. The four-poster bed in this intimate chamber is raised high to provide the two of you with vistas of Avalon village and harbor as well as the California coastline across the channel. The lovely view is also offered from the bathroom, which is equipped with pedestal sink, radiator heater, and a shower/bath with original fixtures, including Mr. Wrigley's extra faucet for regulating an old salt-water system. (It no longer works.) This corner room, which also has a gas fireplace and private bath, is available for around $500.

Two other ocean-view rooms, one with a three-quarter bath and the other with full bath, are also available. One of these, room 6, was formerly a sleeping porch. This small, privately situated corner room holds a double bed and carries a rate of around $300.

When the innkeepers say a full range of guest amenities are offered, they aren't talking about extra blankets and pillows. The self-serve parlor bar is perpetually stocked with cold drinks, and an adjacent table is always heaped with nuts and homemade goodies. Dinner (your names are printed on the souvenir menu) is a delightful, multi-course experience, and the full breakfast is likewise exceptional. And where else is a gas-powered golf cart provided for each guest?

HOTEL VISTA DEL MAR
417 Crescent Avenue (P.O. Box 1979), Avalon, CA
90704
Telephone: (310) 510-1452

Fifteen rooms and suites, each with fireplace, private bathroom, television, and telephone. Continental breakfast served in courtyard. Moderate to deluxe.

GETTING THERE
The hotel is located on Avalon's main street at the heart of the village. Hail a taxi at the boat terminal.

HOTEL VISTA DEL MAR

Avalon

*I*f California has a Mecca for romantics, Catalina Island is it. Whether it's for a honeymoon, anniversary, or weekend splurge, most couples owe it to themselves to make this passion pilgrimage at least once.

While the name Hotel Vista del Mar is among the newer additions to the lodging scene of Avalon, the building has been around for some time. The Vista del Mar is a comparatively upscale hostelry that blossomed from what was known for many years as the Campo Bravo Hotel.

Sporting an open-air atrium and a fresh Mediterranean style, the hotel contains only fifteen rooms, each with tiled wet bar, gas fireplace set in the wall a couple of feet off the floor for romantic viewing from bed, and private tiled bath. Color television, air conditioning, bathrobes, and blow dryer are also found in every room.

Rooms for Romance

If a water view is important, the hotel has two prime bay-vista accommodations, and both are suites (in the low $200 range). These also feature balconies and dual spa tubs placed to take advantage of the view.

The six large deluxe courtyard rooms (mid $100 range) face the atrium and are equipped with queen-sized beds. Smaller rooms are offered in the low to mid $100 range. All the rooms are priced less during the off-season, from November 1–April 30.

"OLD" TURNER INN
232 Catalina Avenue (P.O. Box 97),
Avalon, CA 90704
Telephone: (310) 510-2236

Five rooms, three with full baths; two with three-quarter-size baths; four with fireplaces. Continental breakfast and evening wine and appetizers included. Smoking is not permitted. Moderate to expensive.

GETTING THERE

If you're saddled with luggage, hail an island taxi at the boat terminal for the short ride to the inn. If you've packed light, the walk to the inn is short and pleasant. Walk toward the village along Crescent Avenue and make a left onto Catalina Avenue. The inn is one block up on the left.

"OLD" TURNER INN

Avalon

*F*or visitors to Avalon, we discovered three distinct, romantic alternatives. Those who like to be above it all may opt for the lavish Inn on Mt. Ada. If you prefer being at the heart of the bustling village, there's the Hotel Vista del Mar near the harbor. If you'd like something in between, we suggest a night or two at the quaint "Old" Turner Inn.

Lest you get the idea the "Old" Turner Inn is decrepit, the innkeepers have intentionally placed quotes around the word *old*. True, the venerable structure has been around for more than seventy-five years, but it has been well cared for while providing visitors a chance to sample the Avalon of yesteryear.

Nestled on a residential street only one block from downtown and the harbor beach, the inn functioned as a home until 1987, when the owners, a longtime Avalon family, decided to hang out the welcome sign.

Rooms for Romance

There are five guest rooms, and all but one (the Wicker Room) have woodburning fireplaces. The Garden Room (mid $100 range), the only one on the ground floor, has a king-sized brass-and-iron bed and a three-quarter-size bathroom.

In our opinion, the two most romantic rooms are the front-facing King and Queen suites, both of which have separate, sunny sitting porches with day beds. The King Suite

(mid to upper $100 range) is the inn's largest room and is equipped with walnut antiques, king-sized white iron bed, and full bath. The Queen Suite (mid $100 range) has a queen-sized bed with three-quarter-size bathroom. The inn's two other rooms have full bathrooms. Rates start in the low $100 range.

HOTEL ST. LAUREN
Corner of Metropole and Beacon streets (P.O. Box
497), Avalon, CA 90704
Telephone: (310) 510-2299

Forty-two rooms and mini-suites, each with private
bath, air conditioning, TV, and telephone. Some
have whirlpool tubs and balconies. Continental
breakfast included. Two-night minimum stay on
weekends during high season from late May
through October. Handicapped access. Moderate
to deluxe.

GETTING THERE
The inn is across town from the ferry terminal, so
an island taxi is advised. From the boat terminal,
head north on Crescent Avenue along the beach.
Turn left on Metropole and follow to Beacon. Inn is
on the corner.

HOTEL ST. LAUREN

Avalon

Built in 1987 during the Catalina "renaissance" that brought much-needed new accommodations to the island, the St. Lauren boasts one of the Island's most striking exteriors. The elegant pink and white Victorian-style hotel is bedecked with fancy moldings and balconies. Umbrella-covered tables beckon from the sixth-floor, ocean-view patio.

Inside, the guest rooms are decorated with traditional furnishings, wallcoverings, and draperies. The best rooms face the village and command ocean views.

Rooms for Romance

Room 501 on the fifth floor, offered for around $200, is equipped with a spa tub and shared balcony. This room has one of the hotel's best ocean views.

Room 511, which also commands an ocean vista, is classified as a minisuite, offering a bit more space and a sofa. Minisuites carry rates of around $200. Terry robes are provided in all of the hotel's ocean-view rooms and minisuites.

Unfortunately, some of the guest rooms we visited had the stale odor of cigarette smoke. If you've got a sensitive nose, be sure to communicate your wishes for a nonsmoking room when making a reservation.

The Southern Beach Communities

DAYTIME DIVERSIONS

In Santa Monica, the Third Street Promenade, a popular pedestrian mall two blocks from the Shangri-La, is home to fifty-five restaurants, more than a half-dozen bookstores and numerous specialty shops.

The J. Paul Getty Museum (17985 Pacific Coast Highway) in Malibu is open Tuesday through Sunday.

TABLES FOR TWO

In San Clemente, the Fisherman's Restaurant on San Clemente Pier offers romantic dining over the rolling sea. In Dana Point, the Harbor Grill (seafood) sits on the yacht harbor below the Blue Lantern Inn. Also near the inn is the intimate Luciana's (Italian).

Santa Monica has many dining options, among them Ivy at the Shore, at 1541 Ocean Avenue, and Ocean Avenue Seafood, 1401 Ocean Avenue, both recommended by the Shangri-La staff. Caffe Lido is two houses down the street from Channel Road Inn.

In Malibu, try Wolfgang Puck's striking Granita on West Malibu Road for seafood and pasta. Sand Castle on Pacific Coast Highway is furnished with ocean-view booths. Neptune's Net, also on the coast highway, is a casual dining spot with great chowder and fish-and-chips.

AFTER HOURS

Trancas (30765 Pacific Coast Highway) in Malibu is a popular night spot. There's also a club on the Third Street Promenade in Santa Monica. In Newport Beach, the Oceanfront area is active during the day and evening hours.

CASA TROPICANA

610 Avenida Victoria, San Clemente, CA 92672
Telephone: (714) 492-1234

Nine rooms and suites, each with private bath; all
but Jungle Paradise have gas fireplaces; all but South
Pacific have Jacuzzi tubs for two. Complimentary
breakfast is served on the decks or in your room.
Cantina restaurant on-site. Swimming beach across
the street. Amtrak stops one-hundred feet from the
inn. Secure off-street parking available. Smoking
permitted on outdoor decks only. Rates are lower
from October through April. Moderate to deluxe.

GETTING THERE

From Interstate 5, exit at Avenida Palizada and turn
right. Turn left on El Camino Real, then right on
Del Mar to the pier. The inn is across the street
from the beach.

CASA TROPICANA
San Clemente

We've seen some amazing views from the balconies of California's most romantic retreats, but only at this San Clemente inn were we offered a bird's-eye view of a surfing contest.

A broad, palm-lined lawn is all that separates the ocean from Casa Tropicana, one of the south coast's newest bed-and-breakfast inns. Opened in 1990, the slender, whitewashed Mediterranean-style hostelry offers grand views of surfing contests and beach volleyball games, not to mention those legendary Southern California sunsets.

Building contractor-turned-innkeeper Rick Anderson and his wife Christy are responsible for this laid-back retreat where guests check in at a counter that was once a surfboard. The nine rooms and suites upstairs were designed around a tropical island theme.

Rooms for Romance

Accommodations range from the whimsical to elegant. In Coral Reef (upper $100 range), a large green headboard in the shape of a giant clamshell curves over the pillows of a queen-sized bed. The room also offers a Jacuzzi tub for two and gas fireplace.

A living canopy? In Emerald Forest (mid $100 range), guests slumber under coiled vines growing along the ceiling. Bali Hai offers a mirrored bamboo canopy bed. Both rooms are equipped with tubs for two.

Dark mahogany accessories, Oriental rugs, and oak floors give the Out of Africa suite a rich, romantic look. A stool is provided to aid your ascent to the raised feather bed. Inside the bathroom is a seven-foot-long Jacuzzi tub for two. The room is also equipped with a gas fireplace.

South Pacific, the inn's lowest priced room (low $100 range), is furnished with a queen-sized water bed, fireplace, and refrigerator. Sheet netting is draped over the bed.

The spacious Penthouse (mid $300 range) is a private fifth-floor suite with a huge deck and outdoor Jacuzzi.

Other rooms carry the names Jungle Paradise, Key Largo, and Kokomo. We'll leave the decor to your imagination.

The Casa Tropicana is the only inn we've visited that publishes a brochure with pictures of each room, a full-color romantic menu of sorts. Since each room offers a quite different guest experience, it's worth requesting in advance.

BLUE LANTERN INN
34343 Street of the Blue Lantern, Dana Point, CA
92629
Telephone: (714) 661-1304

Twenty-nine rooms; each with private bath with
double sink, gas fireplace, terry robes, beach towel,
television, telephone, and minirefrigerator stocked
with complimentary refreshments. All but five
rooms have Jacuzzi tubs for two. Complimentary
breakfast (delivered to your room for a $10 per-
couple charge) and afternoon wine and refreshments included. Exercise room on-site; free bicycle
rental available. This is a nonsmoking inn. Handicapped access. Moderate to deluxe.

GETTING THERE
The inn is located one block west of Highway 1 on
Street of the Blue Lantern, twenty minutes south of
the Orange County Airport (John Wayne Airport).

BLUE LANTERN INN
Dana Point

Relaxing in the lobby of the fully booked Blue Lantern Inn one summer Saturday evening, it was difficult to ignore the constant parade of unlucky couples who, lacking reservations, were politely turned away, two-by-two. Only six months new at the time, the Blue Lantern had already attracted quite a following.

Of the growing list of brand new bed-and-breakfast inns springing up along the Southern California coast, the Blue Lantern is perhaps the nicest. Although its bluff-top location prohibits direct beach access, the inn more than makes up for this small disadvantage in decor, amenities, food, and charm.

Sporting an enchanting Cape Cod facade with lots of interesting angles and a gabled slate roof, the Blue Lantern perches at the edge of a Dana Point cliff overlooking the yacht

harbor and coastline. The majestic sailing ship, *Pilgrim*, a 120-foot-long reproduction of town founder Richard Dana's brigantine, is often anchored near the breakwater below.

Rooms for Romance

The Blue Lantern's rooms are described according to their placement. Rooms overlooking Dana Point are offered in the low to mid $100 range. These feature queen-sized or double beds but do not offer ocean views. Rooms with harbor views (mid to high $100 range) have queen-sized or king-sized beds and partial ocean views. Some are equipped with private decks.

The most romantic accommodations are the dozen or so listed as Pacific Edge rooms. These cliffside rooms offer ocean and harbor vistas as well as decks. Rates for these rooms are in the low $200 range.

The fabulous Tower Suite, with thirty-foot-high vaulted ceiling, 180-degree view, telescope, stereo, and balcony, is a favorite among local newlyweds and is often booked months in advance for weekends.

The Blue Lantern's Pacific Edge and Harbor View rooms (not to mention the decadent suite) scored a solid A on our romantic report card. All the ingredients for a passionate escape are in place here: fireplace (although not woodburning), Jacuzzi tub for two (in all but five rooms) in spacious bathrooms that are destinations in themselves, Pacific sunsets, soft quilts, terry robes, and a private breakfast in your room. Ready, set, start packing!

PORTOFINO BEACH HOTEL
2306 West Oceanfront, Newport Beach, CA 92663
Telephone: (714) 673-7030

Seventeen rooms and suites, each with private bath.
Eleven have dual spa tubs; three suites have fireplaces. Continental breakfast included. Amenities
include hair dryers and refrigerators. Parking is
available. Moderate to Deluxe.

GETTING THERE
From Interstate, take Highway 55 toward Newport
Beach. Follow signs to Newport Pier. Hotel is
immediately north of pier, approximately twenty
minutes from John Wayne Airport.

PORTOFINO BEACH HOTEL
Newport Beach

Gazing out to sea from the big brass bed at Portofino Beach Hotel feels almost like being aboard a luxury yacht. With the ocean so close, you half expect to feel the gentle rocking of waves.

Alas, you won't roll with the surf, but your other senses will be overloaded with the stuff of the sea. You can almost taste the moist, salty air.

From the bustling sidewalk and beach out front, the Portofino Beach Hotel is classic Southern California, complete with tiled roof, artsy neon trim, and spindly palms. Inside, however, the owners gutted what was once a store to create a European-style hotel with New World niceties.

Rooms for Romance

Rooms are located on the second floor, and all are richly appointed with antiques, wallpaper, and custom window treatments.

Room 1 offers an unobstructed beach and ocean view. A similar vista is offered from the dual spa tub (with an overhead skylight). Room 2 next door offers much the same setup, without the corner view. Both rooms are priced in the low $200 range. A partial ocean view is offered from room 11 (mid $100 range) which also features a queen-sized bed and skylit, marble spa tub.

The hotel's three sumptuous suites, accessed via a patio walkway at the rear of the building, feature fireplaces, sitting areas, dual spa tubs, and private, ocean-view decks for sunning and kicking back.

DORYMAN'S INN
2102 West Oceanfront, Newport Beach, CA 92663
Telephone: (714) 675-7300

Ten rooms and suites, each with private bathroom,
fireplace, and sunken tub. Continental breakfast
plus egg dish included. Moderate to deluxe.

GETTING THERE
From Interstate 5 take Highway 55 toward Newport
Beach. Follow signs to Newport Pier. Inn is at the
base of pier, approximately twenty minutes from
John Wayne Airport.

D O R Y M A N ' S   I N N
Newport Beach

Contained entirely on the second level of a beachfront building and reached only by a small, private elevator, Doryman's Inn just might be the south coast's best-kept romantic secret.

Rooms for Romance

Unlike some hotels that invest heavily in showy public areas and scrimp on the guest rooms, Doryman's has no grand lobby. The lion's share of attention has been lavished on the impressive bedchambers. All have French glass, antiques, rich draperies, beveled and etched glass mirrors, sexy sunken tubs, tiled fireplaces with carved mantelpieces, brass fixtures, and skylit bathrooms of Italian marble. Beds are canopied and draped with yards and yards of soft fabric.

The best of everything is contained in room 8, the inn's most expensive (in the high $200 range). Features include a king-sized bed, ocean view, and a Jacuzzi tub for two. While all rooms have sunken tubs, only two have spa jets; other tubs are for soaking. Room 6 has the other jets as well as a beautiful king-sized bed with mirrored headboard and access to an outdoor patio.) Room 10 is a two-room suite.

Rooms 1, 2, and 3 have fine ocean views along with the Doryman's standard luxury features. These carry rates in the mid $100 range. Room 5, with ocean view, queen-sized bed, fireplace, and sunken tub, is the inn's least expensive.

If an ocean view is important, be sure to request one of the rooms facing the beach. Some rooms have better views than others.

SEAL BEACH INN AND GARDENS
212 Fifth Street, Seal Beach, CA 90740
Telephone: (213) 493-2416

Twenty-three rooms and suites, each with private
bathroom; two with tubs for two; two with fireplaces. Continental breakfast included. Moderate to
expensive.

GETTING THERE
From Pacific Coast Highway (Highway 1), south on
Fifth Street to inn on left. From San Diego Freeway,
south on Seal Beach Boulevard to Central. Right to
inn at Fifth Street.

SEAL BEACH INN
AND GARDENS
Seal Beach

We first visited this lovely oasis not too long after Marjorie Bettenhausen breathed new life into a tired and aging Seal Beach inn. To say she restored it would give undue credit to the original. It isn't likely the establishment looked this good even on the day it first opened.

It took Ms. Bettenhausen three years to create her vision, and along the way she rediscovered and preserved some of the intrinsic character of the 1920s. Her sweeping decorative and horticultural touches make the Seal Beach Inn a special destination for romantics.

The brick courtyard is cloaked with color. Impatiens, azaleas, and other mature plants fill window boxes and planters. Scalloped blue canopies shade the windows, and handsome wrought-iron railings decorate the steps to many of the rooms. The courtyard also features antique lampposts, a vintage English phone booth, and a two-hundred-year-old fountain.

Rooms for Romance

Privacy-seeking guests prize the Magnolia Villa for its seclusion and sun deck. Behind the solid walnut door (purchased from Universal Studios after "starring" in many movies) is an intimate hideaway with Eastlake furniture, decorated in burgundy and rose hues. The unusual Scottish glass sidelights change color as the lighting shifts.

Bougainvillea is a large, airy room with mahogany furnishings, king-sized bed, and a sitting area with a hand carved, antique velvet-covered couch. There's also a kitchen bar.

A century-plus-year-old bed with a nearly six-foot-high, carved headboard is the dominant fixture of Vienna Woods, which also comes equipped with a blue-tiled tub for two. The tub sits open to the room but can be closed off with a lace shower curtain.

Taking special care of visiting romantics, the inn offers a Gondola Getaway package that combines a night in a special room with a gondola cruise through the nearby canals and Long Beach Harbor.

HOTEL SHANGRI-LA
1301 Ocean Avenue, Santa Monica, CA 90401
Telephone: (310) 394-2791; toll-free (800) 345-7829

Fifty-five rooms and suites, each with private bath, television, and telephone; many with kitchen units and sun decks. Continental breakfast and afternoon tea served daily. Free parking available. Moderate to deluxe.

GETTING THERE
From Interstate 405, exit at Wilshire Boulevard and drive west on Wilshire toward the ocean. Turn left on Ocean. The hotel is at the corner of Ocean and Arizona, three blocks north of the Santa Monica Pier, and across the street from Palisades Park.

HOTEL SHANGRI-LA

Santa Monica

We had been curious about the Shangri-La for some time, having read a few years ago about its immense popularity with celebrities. Our curiosity was also piqued by scenes of the hotel in Randy Newman's rock video, *I Love L.A.*

The trendy set, especially in Southern California, can be as capricious as the wind, but the Shangri-La still enjoys a loyal following. Stevie Nicks, Madonna, Nastassia Kinski, and Diane Keaton have all visited.

Rooms for Romance

A former apartment hotel, the Shangri-La now combines its classic Art Moderne architecture and sleek and simple Deco style with a smattering of vintage reminders of the hotel's earlier days, such as spacious rooms and full kitchens with built-in ironing boards.

The rooms facing Ocean Avenue look out over the Pacific and narrow Palisades Park, probably the south state's most famous park. An ocean sunset is among these rooms' more attractive features. There are also rooms that face the opposite direction, so be sure to specify your preference.

Suite 508 (mid to upper $100 range) is an ocean-view retreat furnished with two king-sized beds, as well as an original Murphy bed (the kind that folds down from the wall).

The bedroom in suite 601 (approximately $200) has an ocean view. This and the other sixth-floor rooms all have private sun decks. Diane Keaton's favorite is suite 600, and Madonna slept in room 607. (If your room doesn't have a private deck you're welcome to use the communal roof patio.)

The top-of-the-line accommodation at Shangri-La is a round penthouse suite (mid $400 range) with two bedrooms and a large private deck.

While we can recommend the Shangri-La as a comfortable, yes, even romantic, place to stay, we must admit to being unable to pinpoint a specific, overriding feature that could help explain its continued drawing power. Maybe it's karma.

CHANNEL ROAD INN
219 West Channel Road, Santa Monica, CA 90402
Telephone: (310) 459-1920

Fourteen rooms and suites, each with private bath
(some have tubs large enough for two). Amenities
include bubble bath, terry robes, telephone, and
flowers. Televisions are available on request. Continental breakfast (can be taken in your room), afternoon wine and cheese, and evening cookies served
daily. Ocean-view spa on-site. Free bicycle rental.
Handicapped access. Moderate to expensive.

GETTING THERE
Follow Interstate 405 west to Pacific Coast Highway (Highway 1). Drive north on the highway to
the third traffic light (Channel Road). Make a hard
right onto Channel Road and drive one-quarter mile
to the inn, on the left.

CHANNEL ROAD INN
Santa Monica

*I*n Santa Monica, we offer readers two considerably different experiences: the uptown, contemporary, multi-story Shangri-La and a historic fourteen-room inn on Channel Road in a beautiful canyon just a few blocks away.

Built in the early 1900s as a family home, the handsome Channel Road Inn is built in shingled Colonial Revival style, somewhat a rarity on the West Coast. The shingles are painted sky blue, and windows are trimmed in white. Guests enter through an ornately carved Craftsman-style door.

Of the fourteen rooms and suites, ten have views of the ocean. (Be aware that Channel Road traffic can be heard from the inn.)

Rooms for Romance

Room 11 (mid $100 range) is decorated in an English garden motif with bleached pine furnishings, including a matching four-poster, queen-sized canopied bed. Guests have a view of the garden and ocean.

Room 12 (mid to upper $100 range) occupies a quiet corner with an ocean view. A cream-and-burgundy color scheme is accented with warm, dark wood. The king-sized bed

has a rattan headboard; from it, guests have an ocean view.

The inn's spacious bridal suite (room 6; high $100 range) is equipped with a four-poster, king-sized canopied bed and lots of Battenburg lace. The separate living room has a nonworking fireplace, comfy sofa, and two lovely Queen Anne chairs. Room 3 has a tub big enough for two—in a pinch.

Our rear corner room, 1, faced the back of the property and opened onto a sunny deck. The small room offered only one chair for relaxing, and the bath was tiny, a pedestal sink squeezed uncomfortably close to the toilet.

MALIBU BEACH INN

22878 Pacific Coast Highway, Malibu, CA 90265

Telephone: (310) 456-6444;

toll-free (800) 4MALIBU.

Forty-seven rooms, each with private bath, television, telephone, videocassette player, wet bar,
honor bar, safe, and hair dryer. All but four rooms
on the first floor have gas fireplaces. Guests have
access to sandy swimming beach. Continental
breakfast can be delivered to guest rooms. Two-
night minimum during summer season; single-night
stays require surcharge. Handicapped access.
Expensive to deluxe.

GETTING THERE

The inn is located on the beach side of the Pacific
Coast Highway (Highway 1), near the Malibu Pier
and Alice's Restaurant, at the north end of town. Los
Angeles International Airport is approximately
thirty-five minutes away. The John Wayne Airport is
about an hour-and-a-half's drive from the inn.

MALIBU BEACH INN

Malibu

Completed in 1989, the Malibu Beach Inn holds the distinction of being the first hotel to be built on this part of the southern coast in forty years. About as close to living in Malibu as most of us will ever get, the inn offers guests a taste of the comfortable life that residents of this exclusive enclave enjoy.

The inn is set so close to the seashore that about all that can be seen from most windows is the blue ocean. Of all our south state destinations, Malibu Beach Inn provides the best access to the Pacific, not to mention some of the choicest views.

Rooms for Romance

Don't expect antiques, flowing fabric, and lace at Malibu Beach Inn. Furnishings here are simple, contemporary, and functional. The layout, similar from room to room, consists of a queen-sized bed; sofa bed; and coffee table facing a tiled gas fireplace with raised hearth; and Philippine-made, cane wall unit housing a wet bar, refrigerator, and drawers. Art is mostly limited to pastel striping and an occasional shell painted on the wall.

Third-level rooms all have vaulted ceilings with recessed lighting, as well as uncovered balconies big enough for a couple of chairs and lounger. Second-level rooms all have covered ocean-view balconies with furniture.

Fireplace rooms are offered for around $200. Pier and ocean-view rooms are available in the mid $150 range. Suites start in the mid $200 range.

The beach is reached via stairs from a tiled patio just outside the lobby. A Continental breakfast is served each morning on the patio or in your room.

LA MER
411 Poli Street, Ventura, CA 93001
Telephone: (805) 643-3600

Five rooms, each with private bath. Amenities
include bathrobes, bubble bath, and complimentary
bottle of wine. Full breakfast included. Moderate to
expensive.

GETTING THERE
From northbound Highway 101, exit at California
Street, turn right off the highway and follow to Poli
Street. Turn left on Poli and follow to inn. From
southbound Highway 101, exit at Main Street and
turn left on Oak Street. Follow to Poli Street. Inn is
on the corner of Poli and Oak.

LA MER
Ventura

Y ou won't find the community of Ventura on too many lists of romantic destinations in the Southland. But don't blame Gisela Baida. As proprietor of a pleasing bed-and-breakfast inn, she has created a cozy, romantic spot in the midst of an otherwise fairly drab commercial environment.

La Mer occupies a pretty hillside spot next to City Hall, overlooking Ventura's historic San Buenaventura business section. A two-story Cape Cod registered as a historical landmark, the Victorian home-turned-inn celebrated its centennial in 1990.

In the refurbishing process, Gisela, a German native, worked to create an inn with an Old World flavor, designing each of the five rooms to reflect the ambience of a specific European country.

Rooms for Romance

In the low $100 range is Captain's Coje, done in a Norwegian nautical theme. Guests sleep on a queen-size, step-up, captain's bed surrounded by nautical objects, including a ship's wheel, a harpoon, and an original deck chair from the *Queen Mary*. The room also has a balcony and private entrance. Like all of the rooms, Captain's Coje has a private bath, and the bed is covered by a European comforter.

Wienerwald (low $100 range), with an Austrian motif, is equipped with a double bed and a sunken tub. This room also has a private entrance.

The centerpiece of the Peter Paul Rubens room (mid $100 range) is a 200-year-old German twin bed set that comes together to create a spacious king-sized bed.

The inn's grandest accommodation (mid $100 range) is Madam Pompadour, a French-style room with a woodburning stove, bay window, balcony with ocean view, and private entry. The bathroom is equipped with an old-fashioned tub on a pedestal.

On the first floor, the Queen Anne, also in the low $100 range, has a bay window with ocean view. Guests should note that the room's private bath, with clawfoot tub, isn't connected to the room; you get to it via the hallway.

A Bavarian buffet breakfast, including Black Forest ham, juice, European cakes, breads, fruits, and cheeses, is served in the sunny breakfast room.

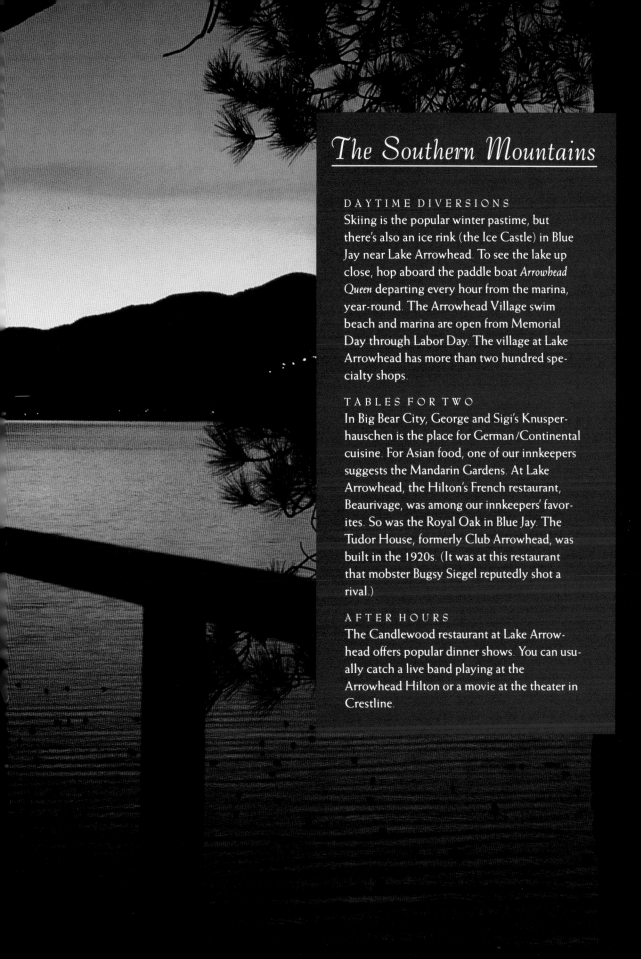

The Southern Mountains

DAYTIME DIVERSIONS

Skiing is the popular winter pastime, but there's also an ice rink (the Ice Castle) in Blue Jay near Lake Arrowhead. To see the lake up close, hop aboard the paddle boat *Arrowhead Queen* departing every hour from the marina, year-round. The Arrowhead Village swim beach and marina are open from Memorial Day through Labor Day. The village at Lake Arrowhead has more than two hundred specialty shops.

TABLES FOR TWO

In Big Bear City, George and Sigi's Knusper-hauschen is the place for German/Continental cuisine. For Asian food, one of our innkeepers suggests the Mandarin Gardens. At Lake Arrowhead, the Hilton's French restaurant, Beaurivage, was among our innkeepers' favorites. So was the Royal Oak in Blue Jay. The Tudor House, formerly Club Arrowhead, was built in the 1920s. (It was at this restaurant that mobster Bugsy Siegel reputedly shot a rival.)

AFTER HOURS

The Candlewood restaurant at Lake Arrowhead offers popular dinner shows. You can usually catch a live band playing at the Arrowhead Hilton or a movie at the theater in Crestline.

GOLD MOUNTAIN MANOR
1117 Anita (P.O. Box 2027),
Big Bear City, CA 92314
Telephone: (714) 585-6997

Seven rooms, one with full private bath; two with
half-baths. Six rooms have fireplaces or woodburning stoves. Full breakfast and afternoon refreshments included. Two-night minimum stay on
weekends and holidays. Moderate to expensive.

GETTING THERE
From San Bernardino, take Highway 330 to Run-
ning Springs, where it becomes Highway 18. Drive
east to Big Bear Dam. Stay left around dam onto
Highway 38 (North Shore Drive), following sign to
Fawnskin. Seven miles past Fawnskin, turn left on
Anita to inn.

GOLD MOUNTAIN MANOR
Big Bear City

To many traveling romantics, a guest room without private bath is like a rosebush without a bloom. In identifying south state romantic getaways, we treated private bathrooms as a basic prerequisite. But there are exceptions to every rule.

We fudged a bit by including Gold Mountain Manor (only one room has a full private bath) because of its popularity and romantic history. You see, among the inn's cozy furnishings is the woodstove that reputedly warmed the toes of film legends Clark Gable and Carole Lombard during their honeymoon at Gable's Big Bear retreat.

The log-walled manor house is all that remains of a once thriving, private resort. Set among the pines three miles from the lake, the house was built to the high standards of the rich and famous who frequented the area.

Rooms for Romance

The Clark Gable Room (low $100 range) is one of the most popular of the inn's rooms. The room is furnished with French walnut antiques, and there's a cozy alcove. Fans of Gable and Lombard might be willing to overlook the absence of a private bath for a chance to stoke the Franklin woodburning stove that Cark and Carole used. The cozy shared bath is directly across the hall, so at least you won't have to trek too far.

The Presidential Suite (mid $150 range) is the only room with a full private bath. Decorated in country French, the room featues a four-poster bed, river-rock fireplace, and private access.

A spa tub for two is the main attraction of the rustic Ted Ducey Room (half-bath; mid $100 range), formerly the garage, situated a few steps down from the main level. The only other room with a half-bath (sink and toilet) is the Honeymoon Room, with wicker furnishings, stained-glass fireplace, and netting over the bed.

There are two shared bathrooms in the house. One is furnished with vintage fixtures, including a clawfoot tub and pedestal sink. The other is a large modern bath.

While you'll probably be spending most of your time here behind closed doors, the inn's rustic and cozy public areas are noteworthy.

WINDY POINT INN
39263 North Shore Drive (P.O. Box 375), Fawnskin,
CA 92333
Telephone: (714) 866-2746

Four rooms, each with private bath, fireplace, refrigerator, ceiling fan, stereo cassette player, and lake/
mountain view; one room with tub for two. Television, videocassette player, exercise equipment, and
spa on-site. Boat dock available. Complimentary
breakfast may be taken in your room. Afternoon
refreshments served daily. Midweek rates are lower.
This is a nonsmoking inn. Handicapped access.
Moderate to deluxe.

GETTING THERE
From San Bernardino, take Highway 330 to Run-
ning Springs where it becomes Highway 18. Follow
Highway 18 to Big Bear Dam. Veer toward the left
at the dam and follow Highway 38 (North Shore
Drive) two miles to the inn.

WINDY POINT INN
Fawnskin

There's nothing like a view of a beautiful mountain lake to ignite romantic sparks, and we're not aware of a better place from which to savor the panorama of Big Bear Lake than Windy Point Inn, located on the quiet north shore.

The inn, which could pass for a large mountain home, is placed among pines on a breezy, private peninsula just steps from the water's edge. Two sandy beaches are close by.

Built in 1990, the chalet-style inn contains only four bedrooms. Each is equipped with its own bathroom and woodburning fireplace. The downstairs common area has a sunken lake-view living room with corner woodburning stove. A grand piano sits nearby on a polished hardwood floor.

Rooms for Romance

It would be difficult, if not impossible, to imagine a room more romantic than The Peaks, Windy Point's largest and most expensive accommodation (mid $200 range). A large wrap-around sofa sits in front of the fireplace; the king-sized bed is situated under a skylight for star gazing; there's a private deck for lake gazing; and a spa tub for two offers incredible vistas from a picture window (there's also a skylight above the tub). Lights are controlled by a rheostat, and the lake can be seen from all the windows. Completing the scene are a double shower and glass-walled steam sauna, and a CD and cassette stereo with six-speaker surround sound.

At the other end of the rate schedule is Sands (mid $100 range), a comparatively small room but also favored by visiting romantics. The lake view from the private deck is particularly inspiring.

Pines (mid to upper $100 range) is a split-level retreat with vaulted ceiling, kitchenette, and private deck. Guests here also enjoy private outside access. Cliffs, a studio lake-view suite, also has a kitchenette and outdoor entrance. It features a beamed ceiling and bathroom skylight.

At night, during winter, lights from the ski resort across the lake flicker on the water. During summer months, the moon's reflection on the glassy surface lulls guests relaxing on the inn's decks.

KNICKERBOCKER MANSION
869 South Knickerbocker (P.O. Box 3661), Big Bear
Lake Village, CA 92315
Telephone: (714) 866-8221

Ten rooms, five with private bath; one with woodburning stove and tub for two. Outdoor spa on-site.
Expanded Continental breakfast buffet and evening
refreshments included. Smoking permitted outdoors only. Two-night minimum stay on weekends;
three- and four-night minimum during holiday
periods. Moderate to expensive.

GETTING THERE
From San Bernardino, take Highway 330 to Run-
ning Springs, where it becomes Highway 18. Follow through Big Bear Lake Village and turn right on
Knickerbocker Road. The inn is on the left, a
quarter-mile south of Big Bear Lake Village.

KNICKERBOCKER MANSION
Big Bear Lake Village

*T*he rustic Knickerbocker Mansion is a 1920s-era log-walled mountain manor house, with the logs placed vertically and joined with white plaster. Built by Big Bear's first damkeeper, Bill Knickerbocker, the striking three-story home is set on an expanse of lawn and surrounded by evergreens. The estate makes for an especially enchanting scene with a frosting of snow.

Rooms for Romance

For purposes of this book, we're limiting our romantic recommendation in the main house to the spacious suite (mid $150 range) that comprises the third floor (and those enchanting gables). A bed sits in one of the gables; the other holds a separate sitting area with wrap-around couch facing a giant-screen television with videocassette player. The suite also features a woodburning stove, a private bath with spa tub for two, as well as a microwave, refrigerator, and CD stereo player.

Adjacent to the handsome main house and facing the forest is the estate's original barn, since refurbished and renamed Rainbow Sun Lodge. Inside are four loft rooms with private baths (low $100 range).

WAINWRIGHT INN
43113 Moonridge Road (P.O. Box 130406), Big Bear
Lake, CA 92315
Telephone: (714) 585-6914

Four rooms, two with private baths. Full gourmet
breakfast and afternoon wine and cheese included;
complimentary snacks available in common area.
Television and videocassette player on-site. This is a
nonsmoking inn. Free shuttle service to and from ski
resort is provided. Two-night minimum stay on
weekends and three- to four-night minimum on
holidays. Moderate to expensive.

GETTING THERE
From San Bernardino, take Highway 330 to Run-
ning Springs, where it becomes Highway 18. Follow Highway 18 through Big Bear Lake Village.
Turn left at the three-way stop sign and then right
at the traffic light onto Big Bear Boulevard. Turn
right at the next light (Moonridge Road) and follow
for one-and-a-half miles to the inn, on the right.

WAINWRIGHT INN
Big Bear

*A*t many upscale inns and small hotels, we've been more than a bit surprised by the hefty rates demanded for honeymoon suites. After touring many fancy love nests that fetch well over $200 a night, we were excited to stumble upon one of the southern mountain region's most romantic rooms for lovers on a budget. It's also the closest lodging to Bear Mountain ski resort.

Rooms for Romance

At Wainwright Inn, you and yours may luxuriate in the Honeymoon Hideaway, complete with wet bar, gas fireplace, romantic sleigh bed, and spa tub for two, all for a rate in the mid $100 range. This room, located on the main floor, also has its own entrance.

The honeymooners' retreat is one of four rooms in this large, contemporary Tudor-style home-turned-inn. The only other private bath is in the Tudor Rose Suite (low to mid $100 range). The suite features a draped and canopied four-poster bed, antique and reproduction Victorian furniture, window seat with leaded glass, vaulted ceiling, and separate sitting area with wet bar.

If you don't mind sharing a bath (maybe you're traveling with another couple), the nicely decorated Empire Room and Contessa Room on the second floor are also available (for around $100).

CHATEAU DU LAC
911 State Highway 173 (P.O. Box 1098), Lake
Arrowhead, CA 92352
Telephone: (714) 337-6488

Six rooms, four with private baths; one with fireplace; three with tubs for two. All rooms have televisions, telephones, and queen-sized beds. Full
breakfast and afternoon refreshments included. This
is a nonsmoking inn. Moderate to deluxe.

GETTING THERE
From San Bernardino, take Highway 18 to Lake
Arrowhead. At the signal, turn right on Highway
173 and drive three miles to Hospital Road. Turn
right; the inn is the first house on the right.

CHATEAU DU LAC
Lake Arrowhead

*J*ust prior to wrapping up our south state romantic inn-vestigations, we were fortunate to hear about Chateau du Lac, a new inn at Lake Arrowhead, allegedly a paradise for lovers. A lucky break. As it turned out, the chateau emerged as one of the most romantic retreats in the southern mountains.

When innkeepers Oscar and Jody Wilson happened by here in 1988, the structure was being built as a house. The Wilsons took over, made some modifications, and finished it as an elegant mountain inn.

A beautifully eclectic mix of styles employing clapboard, stone, brick, and artful white trim, Chateau du Lac occupies a heavenly spot on the lake, opposite the village, whose distant lights twinkle at night.

Rooms for Romance

The Loft Room (high $100 range) is a comfortable suite containing a sitting room, a Jacuzzi tub (for one), and private entrance for discreet comings and goings.

On the uppermost level of the inn is an intimate suite with television and reading alcove and Jacuzzi tub for two (high $100 range). Another bedroom with private bath is located on the inn's main floor. Two bedrooms on the lower level share a bathroom.

The Lakeview Room (mid $200 range) is a seductive showplace, and quite possibly the most beautiful guest room in the southern mountains. Open beams and trusses form a *V* over the room, furnished with brick fireplace, lace curtains, and rich antiques. Walls are

covered with delicately flowered wallpaper. Chocolate brown carpeting contrasts with the bed's soft white coverlet. There's also a Jacuzzi tub for two and a balcony overlooking the lake.

The views of the lake from this and other of the chateau's rooms will blow your socks off, along with a few other garments.

The Desert

DAYTIME DIVERSIONS

In the desert, daytime activities are somewhat seasonal. During the winter months, when the weather is often in the comfortable seventy-degree range, visitors can be found on the golf course (there were about seventy at last count), tennis court (more than four-hundred), or shopping on fashionable El Paseo in Palm Desert.

In the summertime, when the mercury regularly pushes the century mark, the downtown cafes turn on their misting machines and the Oasis Waterpark on Gene Autry Trail does a brisk business. Other visitors prefer air-conditioned pursuits like shopping at Palm Springs' Desert Fashion Plaza or ice skating at the Palm Desert Town Center. Although it's a worthwhile experience any time of year, a summer ride up the Palm Springs Aerial Tramway to a cool elevation of 8,500 feet provides refreshing relief from the desert heat. The tram entrance is on Highway 111 and Tramway Road.

TABLES FOR TWO

Our innkeepers recommended the intimate French bistro, Chez Zizi (276 North Palm Canyon Drive), Cuistot (El Paseo), and, for great Italian dishes, Riccio's (2155 North Palm Canyon Drive). At Dar Maghreb (300 Bob Hope Drive, Rancho Mirage) you'll sit on cushioned sofas while sampling Moroccan cuisine. Las Casuelas (368 North Palm Canyon Drive, Palm Springs) has been a local Mexican food favorite since 1958.

AFTER HOURS

Although many stores are closed at night, window shopping along trendy Palm Canyon Drive is an enjoyable way to spend a warm Palm Springs evening. Along the way you'll discover cafes and ice cream shops for dessert. And if the weather's cooperative, how about a moonlight swim in the pool at your inn?

INGLESIDE INN
200 West Ramon Road (at Belardo), Palm Springs,
CA 92262
Telephone: toll-free (800) 772-6655

Twenty-nine rooms and suites, each with private
bathroom; 12 with fireplaces; some with sunken
tubs. All have personal-size whirlpool and steam
bathtubs. Amenities include bathrobes, bubble
bath, monogrammed matchbooks, fresh fruit, and
refrigerators stocked with free snacks and drinks.
Complimentary Continental breakfast brought to
your door, along with daily newspaper and the inn's
own weather report. Complimentary limousine service available. Melvyn's restaurant, lounge, pool,
and spa on site. Moderate to deluxe.

GETTING THERE
From Interstate 10, exit at Ramon Road, and follow
into Palm Springs. The inn is tucked privately at the
edge of downtown, a block west of Palm Canyon
Drive at the corner of Ramon and Belardo. Palm
Springs is one hundred miles from Los Angeles.

INGLESIDE INN
Palm Springs

When current owner Mel Haber began refurbishing Palm Springs' classic Ingleside Inn in the mid-1970s he discovered a titillating bit of Hollywood history tucked away in the cluttered office. In a dusty box he found a juicy card file chronicling the private lives of some of the world's most famous celebrities.

Original owner Ruth Hardy enjoyed playing hostess to Gable and Lombard, who honeymooned here, as well as the likes of Greta Garbo, John Wayne, and Rita Hayworth. However, according to the historic archives, guests were only welcome if they measured up to Ms. Hardy's quirky standards.

Judging from the secret file, not every well-known guest earned the Ingleside stamp of approval. If you were too blond, too brassy, too big or too small, or if you snuck in for an illicit rendezvous, chances are Ms. Hardy's dossier would have labeled you "NG," meaning no good, or "definitely not our type." Howard Hughes failed the Hardy test when, according to the innkeeper's notes, he and starlet Ava Gardner slipped into a cozy villa here under assumed names.

Today, a pampered, casual elegance pervades the rambling Spanish-style inn, although many of the antique chairs and sofas were in need of reupholstery at the time of our last visit.

Rooms for Romance

Princess (room 148) is a favorite among honeymooners and serious romantics. The floor is made of white paving stones, and there's a fireplace and white, king-sized canopied bed.

Another popular retreat is the Lily Pons Room (room 143), where the famous diva actually lived for some time. The room features French provincial design and a private patio. The Princess and Lily Pons rooms carry nightly rates in the high $200 range.

The Royal Suite (villa 8) is a two-room retreat with two gas fireplaces, two baths, a sunken tub (for one person), and a king-sized bed with antique Spanish headboard.

Among the rooms with the lowest rates are room 138 (low $100 range) and room 139 (around $100). Both face a garden and are very private.

The Penthouse units (around $100) offer views of the San Jacinto Mountains (pronounced ha-SEEN-toe), the nearby range that casts early evening shade over the lush, well-manicured gardens of the inn.

VILLA ROYALE
1620 Indian Trail, Palm Springs, CA 92264
Telephone: (619) 327-2314; or toll-free (800) 245-
2314

Thirty-three rooms, suites, studios, and villas, several with fireplaces, private spas, and patios. Each
room has a television and telephone; many have
fully equipped kitchens. Complimentary Continental breakfast served poolside (or in your room, during winter season). Restaurant on-site is open
during winter season. Two swimming pools, one
spa, bar, and piano lounge on-site. Complimentary
morning newspaper and bicycle rental. Handicapped access. Moderate to deluxe.

GETTING THERE
From Interstate 10, exit at Highway 11 (Palm
Springs) to center of town. Veer right at the down-
town split in the road onto East Palm Canyon
Drive. Turn left on Indian Trail and follow to inn.

VILLA ROYALE
Palm Springs

Although dozens and dozens of hotels and motels line the main thoroughfares from one end of Palm Springs to the other, we found the real gems only by poking around the side streets. Among these hidden treasures is Villa Royale, one of Palm Springs' best-kept secrets.

From its early days as a 1930s-era private home, the property has grown to thirty-three antique-furnished guest rooms and two swimming pools spread over more than three lushly landscaped acres.

Rooms for Romance

The tile-roofed guest wings are situated around a series of four courtyards framed by pillars, arches, shade trees, potted plants, and cascading Bougainvillea. There's even a fountain courtyard where passersby are serenaded with classical music. (Room 103 is closest to the musical fountain.)

For the most privacy, we suggest the rooms 201 through 205, if available. These face a quiet fountain courtyard well removed from the public areas.

Room 203 (mid $100 range), a one-bedroom corner suite facing a fountain courtyard, features a French theme and holds a king-sized bed and fireplace. The bathroom is reached via a pretty leaded-glass door. The room is equipped with a small dining room as well as an intimate kitchen. At another corner of the courtyard is room 201, an oft-requested retreat with private spa (mid $100 range). Eight rooms have private two-person spas.

The inn's most remote accommodations, rooms 301 through 309, face the swimming pool farthest from the dining room and office. One of the largest and most unusual rooms is 305 (low $100 range), containing a trove of antique items that include a squad of wooden toy soldiers and a family of toy bears placed in an old wooden wheelbarrow. Two facing love seats sit before a large brick fireplace. A beamed cathedral ceiling runs the length of the room, from the king-sized bed to a small serving bar, next to a spacious kitchen. The private patio is shaded by an olive tree.

The inn has few rules, but two are commendable. You won't be bothered by blaring music while you relax by the pool. Radios aren't allowed, unless they're connected to a headset. Also, since there are no posted swimming pool and spa hours, you can take a midnight dip, as long as you're quiet.

CASA CODY

175 South Cahuilla Road, Palm Springs, CA 92262
Telephone: toll-free (800) 231-CODY.

Seventeen rooms and suites, each with private bath,
television, and telephone; some with kitchens and
fireplaces. Continental breakfast included. Two
swimming pools and tree-shaded spa-on site. Two-
night minimum stay required most weekends; three-
night minimum during most holiday periods. Handicapped access. Inexpensive to moderate.

GETTING THERE

From Interstate 10, exit at Highway 111 (becomes
Palm Canyon Drive) and follow into Palm Springs.
Turn right on Tahquitz Canyon Way and take sec-
ond left on South Cahuilla.

CASA CODY
Palm Springs

*H*aving learned in advance of our visit that Casa Cody was one of the oldest inns in Palm Springs and that the original owner was related to Buffalo Bill Cody, we had visions of crumbling adobe walls and gardens of aging cactus. Then we discovered that this resort area became popular only well after the turn of the century, and that founder Harriet Cody was Buffalo Bill's niece. Compared to some historic inns we've visited, the 1920s-era Casa Cody is a youngster.

Having staked an early claim to one of the choicest spots, the inn is nicely situated at the base of the San Jacinto mountains and only a short walk from downtown shops and restaurants. As the sun sets behind the mountains, Casa Cody is among the first Palm Springs hostelries to enjoy cooler evening shade.

The single-story inn is modest, simple, and cozy. It grew recently with the acquisition of an adjacent motel, and now includes two swimming pools and seventeen rooms and suites. Rates here are among the most reasonable of all our recommended romantic retreats in Palm Springs, starting well under $100 per night during the high season (late December through April). High-season rates for Casa Cody's nicest suites top out at the mid $100 level.

Rooms for Romance

Remodeled fairly recently, the inn's rooms feature handmade, Santa Fe-style pine furniture and terra-cotta floors covered by colorful rugs. Many have fireplaces and kitchens. French doors provide lots of sunlight.

Suite 5 takes advantage of a beautiful mountain view and has a patio from which to savor the scene. It's also equipped with kitchen.

Suite 6 has a living room with fireplace, separate bedroom, and kitchen, while suite 7 has similar features and an additional bedroom. All suites have tiled kitchens; rooms are equipped with small refrigerators.

SUNDANCE VILLAS

303 Cabrillo Road, Palm Springs, CA 92262
Telephone: (619) 325-3888

Nineteen two- and three-bedroom/two- and three-bath villas, each equipped with private pool and spa, fireplace, tub for two, television, video player, sound system, wet bar, full kitchen with accessories, and gas barbeque. Most have washers and dryers. Common area has pool/spa and lighted tennis court. Continental breakfast included on arrival morning; fresh fruit and champagne provided on arrival. Room service and massage services available. Nonsmoking villas available. Checkout time, 1 p.m. Two-night minimum stay required. Villas will accommodate wheelchairs; management will assist with other adaptive arrangements for disabled guests. Deluxe.

GETTING THERE

Sundance Villas is located between Indian Avenue and Palm Canyon Drive, one block north of Racquet Club Road, adjacent to Palm Springs Racquet Club. From Interstate 10, exit at Highway 111 (Palm Springs). Turn left on Yorba Road, right on De Anza, and left on Cabrillo to resort.

S U N D A N C E   V I L L A S
Palm Springs

Only in a desert paradise like Palm Springs could travelers hope to find a resort with a private pool and spa for every room. At Sundance Villas, one of two such resorts we discovered, the nineteen, two- and three-bedroom villas are all privately owned vacation retreats, each equipped with its own outdoor spa and pool. One of the three-bedroom units, Villa Victoria, is owned by actress Victoria Principal. A Hollywood producer also owns one. Other celebrity owners prefer anonymity.

Rooms for Romance

Each villa is equipped with a kitchen and a living area with television, video player, sound system, fireplace, and wet bar. Bathrooms feature three-by-eight-foot tubs for two. Six-foot-high fences ensure privacy.

One of the most romantic of the resort's villas is Shangri-La, which boasts an oversized master suite with wet bar and fireplace (there's another fireplace in the living area), his-and-her baths (hers has the tub for two), and a pretty deck.

Arranged duplex style, the villas are built around a common garden and recreation area with tennis court and pool/spa.

High-season rates (January through May) range from the mid to high $300 range for a two-bedroom villa to around $500 for a deluxe three-bedroom unit. In the off-season, rates drop considerably.

If Sundance Villas' rates are beyond your budget, consider the economical alternative of inviting another couple, renting a two-bedroom pool villa (mid $300 range and higher during the high season), and sharing the cost.

By the way, in the (unlikely) event you tire of your private paradise, there's a central pool/spa a few steps away.

LA MANCHA PRIVATE VILLAS AND COURT CLUB

444 Avenida Caballeros at Alejo (P.O. Box 340),
Palm Springs, CA 92263
Telephone: (619) 323–1773; toll-free in California,
(800) 255-1773

Fifty villas, many with fireplaces, private pools, and
spas. Amenities, in addition to those described
above, include bathrobes, hair dryers, refrigerators,
VCRs, and food basket on arrival. Expensive to
deluxe (November through May) and deluxe (May
through October).

GETTING THERE

From Interstate 10, exit at Highway 111 (Palm
Springs) to center of town. Left on Amado, five
blocks to Avenida Caballeros. Left to resort. You'll
be issued a gate key card at check in.

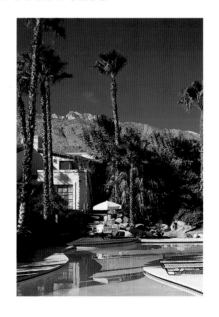

LA MANCHA PRIVATE VILLAS
AND COURT CLUB
Palm Springs

We couldn't think of a better climax for our passionate pass through the desert than a stay at La Mancha, quite possibly the southland's ultimate romantic destination.

Set up like a small, exclusive village, La Mancha is actually a private club that's open to ordinary folks like us. An oasis in the most romantic sense, La Mancha includes fifty Spanish- and Moroccan-style casitas and villas with some eighteen different floor plans. These luxury accommodations range from one-bedroom and one-bath units to those with three bedrooms, three baths, and den. Some have split levels; others are two-story with lofts. They also come with (or without) private walled-in spa, swimming pool, and/or tennis court.

Rooms for Romance

Our two-bedroom villa, which offered all the conveniences of a small luxury home, had televisions in both bedrooms, queen-sized beds, and two bathrooms (one with a bidet). In the step-down living room was a large-screen television with video disc player, an elaborate sound system, couch and love seat, and a tiled and mirrored fireplace. The villa also contained a full kitchen (with dishes, cutlery, and pots and pans), dining room, and a washer and dryer.

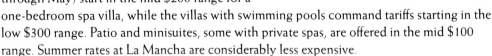

French doors opened to the *piece de resistance*: our own pool, four or five feet deep, along with extras like a spacious, connected spa, covered wet bar, table and chairs, gas barbecue, and plenty of patio furniture. Six-foot-high walls separated us from the neighbors, providing total privacy, so don't bother bringing bathing suits. However, don't forget the sunscreen for those, er, sensitive areas.

Daily high-season rates (November through May) start in the mid $200 range for a one-bedroom spa villa, while the villas with swimming pools command tariffs starting in the low $300 range. Patio and minisuites, some with private spas, are offered in the mid $100 range. Summer rates at La Mancha are considerably less expensive.

At the time of our visit, the resort was offering a three-night Romantic Interlude package that included a spa villa for around $800 or pool villa for around $900, with private dinner served in your room, breakfast, and use of tennis courts and bikes.

The resort is also equipped with a gymnasium, large club pool, paddle tennis and tournament tennis courts, and a croquet court. A convertible from La Mancha's "sun fleet" is also available at a reasonable rate.

The San Diego Area

DAYTIME DIVERSIONS
Two of San Diego's most popular attractions
are within walking distance of the Horton
Grand Hotel. Horton Plaza shopping center
on Island Avenue is a multilevel shopping center located between Third and Fourth avenues.
Seaport Village, a fourteen-acre shopping and
restaurant complex, runs along the harbor.
The San Diego Convention Center is also a
short walk away.

A little farther away is Old Town State His-
toric Park which offers a glimpse of early San
Diego. And don't forget the famous San Diego
Zoo (and Wild Animal Park), Sea World, and
Balboa Park.

TABLES FOR TWO
In Carlsbad, Neiman's restaurant (Carlsbad
Village Drive) is housed in a beautiful Victo-
rian mansion that was home to the town
founder. Henry's, also on Carlsbad Village
Drive, was recommended by our innkeepers.

PELICAN COVE INN
320 Walnut Avenue, Carlsbad, CA 92008
Telephone: (619) 434-5995

Eight rooms and suites, each with feather bed, private bath, gas fireplace, and television (phone available on request); four have tubs for two. Complimentary Continental breakfast may be taken to your room. Beach access two-hundred yards away. Two-night minimum stay required on weekends and holiday periods. Handicapped access. Moderate to expensive.

GETTING THERE
From Interstate 5, exit at Carlsbad Village Drive. Drive west to Carlsbad Boulevard; south three blocks to Walnut and east to inn.

PELICAN COVE INN

Carlsbad

A century ago, Carlsbad earned a fair amount of notoriety after the accidental discovery of curative water under the village. In recent years, however, the spotlight has shifted away from this quaint village, shining more brightly on the trendy streets of nearby La Jolla.

Weekending San Diegans and others who have been lucky enough to discover Carlsbad's Pelican Cove Inn would probably prefer that we kept this romantic destination to ourselves. But we couldn't resist.

Attorney Bob Hale and his wife, Celeste, a court reporter, crafted the charming, light-blue inn in 1987 from a couple of little apartment complexes. Located just a couple of hundred yards from the beach, the Pelican Cove has since doubled in size with the construction of an adjacent two-story unit that houses four large rooms.

Rooms for Romance

From the street, the most eye-catching feature of the inn is an octagonal wing, the bottom level of which serves as the public room. On the second story is the intimate Newport Room (low $100 range), where a queen-sized brass feather bed sits under the windowed octagon dome.

In Carlsbad (low $100 range), a high king-sized bed dominates the room. There's also a brass-and-iron day bed and a skylight.

There are four spacious rooms in Pelican Cove's new building. La Jolla, the inn's nicest (mid $100 range), boasts a high, rounded ceiling and champagne-and-black color scheme. In the bathroom is a spa tub for two.

Coronado, another of the new accommodations (mid $100 range), has a draped, four-poster, king-sized bed. The bathroom holds a spa tub for two. The room is decorated in hues of peach and seafoam green.

For guests who can't bear to leave the inn on a nice day, the owners have created a sun deck atop the second floor.

THE BED AND BREAKFAST INN AT LA JOLLA

7753 Draper Avenue, La Jolla, CA 92037

Telephone: (619) 456-2066

Sixteen rooms, all but one with private baths; some with twin beds. Three with fireplaces; three with two-person tubs. Amenities include bubble bath, sherry and fresh fruit in rooms, and evening wine and cheese tasting. Continental breakfast of pastries, muffins, and juice is served in your room, the dining room, or the garden. Two-night minimum stay during weekends. Moderate to deluxe.

GETTING THERE

From Interstate 5, exit at La Jolla Village Drive west. Turn left on Torrey Pines Road, right on Prospect through town to Draper. The inn sits between La Jolla Presbyterian Church and the Women's Club.

THE BED & BREAKFAST INN AT LA JOLLA

La Jolla

We made a special point of visiting the Bed and Breakfast Inn at La Jolla on an early mid-week afternoon. The inn is often solidly booked on weekends, and we wanted to see, in person, as many as possible of the seductive-looking rooms pictured in the inn's brochure.

The hardwood squeaked underfoot as we explored the hallways of the early 1900s-era Cubist mansion, home for a time to the family of composer John Philip Sousa. Ten rooms are located in the main house. Six have been added in a newer adjoining building.

Rooms for Romance

Among the more affordable is Country Village (low $100 range), a spacious room with sitting area decorated in blue. Garden is a handsome room done in Ralph Lauren plaid, with fireplace and clawfoot tub.

Holiday (high $100 range), a large corner room, has a draped and canopied four-poster, king-sized bed that sits before a fireplace. There's also a separate sitting area and private bath with tub for two. Fiesta and Irving Gill Penthouse also feature tubs for two.

For those with a yearning to see the ocean, Pacific View (mid $100 range) offers the best view, along with a fireplace.

HORTON GRAND HOTEL

311 Island Avenue, San Diego, CA 92101. Telephone: (619) 544-1886. One-hundred-and-ten rooms, each with private bath, gas fireplace, television, telephone, and air conditioning. Restaurant and bar on-site. Honeymoon packages, including a horse-drawn carriage ride, are available. Moderate to deluxe.

GETTING THERE

The Horton Grand is located two blocks from Horton Plaza shopping center on Island Avenue, between Third and Fourth Avenues. From Interstate 5 (northbound), exit at Sixth avenue and drive to Fourth Avenue. Turn left on Fourth, and right on Island. From San Diego Freeway (southbound), exit at Front avenue and drive to Market. Turn left on Market, right on Fourth and right on Island. Seaport Village shops and the San Diego Convention Center are a short walk away.

HORTON GRAND HOTEL
San Diego

We've heard of the earth moving during a romantic encounter, but walls shaking and pictures turning? Some claim it has happened at Horton Grand Hotel, but not necessarily during the heat of passion. The strange goings on in room 309 are reportedly the work of a mischievous ghost named Roger, who makes his presence known from time to time.

Since its opening over a hundred years ago, the venerable Horton Grand has come a long way. A couple of blocks, to be precise. It once stood on the site of San Diego's famous Horton Plaza and was moved, in thousands of pieces, down the street by forward-thinking developers bent on preserving a slice of San Diego history.

The resurrected structure is actually two hotels in one: the Horton Grand and the Kahle Saddlery Hotel, another century-old local hostelry that likewise had been targeted for demolition.

The Horton Grand of today is a luxurious lovers' oasis in the heart of San Diego's downtown. Its Cowboy Victorian decor has given way to antiques, platformed and draped beds, lace curtains, and cozy gas fireplaces with marble mantels.

Rooms for Romance

Although the hotel itself is a gem, parts of the neighborhood have not yet been rejuvenated. Consequently, most of the rooms facing the city do not boast inspiring views. Our advice is to request a third- or fourth-floor Palace room or suite with a balcony facing the lovely interior brick courtyard (low to mid $100 range). The white wrought-iron balconies and mature shade trees are reminiscent of New Orleans' French Quarter.

In each of the Horton Grand's accommodations, you'll find platformed queen-sized beds and ceiling fans, as well as a room journal with descriptions of romantic liaisons of former guests. Although some are candid enough to make a San Diego sailor blush, most of the diary entries are innocent, heartfelt reflections about rediscovering romance or savoring a long overdue getaway from the daily grind.

By the way, if you're among the many interested in spending the night in Roger's Room, better make your reservation soon. There's a several-month-long wait to spend a night in room 309 with, or without, the resident ghost.

Note: Just prior to going to press, we learned that the Horton Grand has added two dozen suites, each with antiques, two telephones, two televisions, wet bar, and microwave.

RANCHO VALENCIA RESORT
P.O. Box 9126, Rancho Santa Fe, CA 92067
Telephone: (619) 756-1123

Forty-three rooms and suites, each with private
bathroom, fireplace, tub for two, two televisions,
and telephone. Amenities (these vary according to
the rate) include fresh flowers, bathrobes, complimentary bottle of wine, and safes. Fresh orange
juice, newspaper, and rose delivered to your room in
the morning. Complimentary Continental buffet
breakfast served daily in dining room. Swimming
pool and spa, tennis courts, and croquet course on-
site. Guests have golf privileges at a nearby course.
Handicapped access. Deluxe.

GETTING THERE
From Interstate 5, exit at Del Mar Heights Road and
drive east. Turn left on El Camino Real and drive for
three miles. Turn right on San Diegueno and drive
for three miles. Turn right on Rancho Diegueno,
and then make an immediate left on Rancho Valencia Road. Then turn left on Rancho Valencia Drive.

Rancho Santa Fe

*I*t's hard to believe this remote hilltop resort is only twenty-five minutes from bustling downtown San Diego. The madding crowd might as well be a million miles away.

Situated above a quiet, upscale suburb of equestrian estates, the resort was planned for those who seek privacy. The public areas are well distanced from most of the suites and rooms, so you won't encounter other guests unless you want to. However, the palm-crowned pool area is only a short walk away.

Rooms for Romance

The resort consists of twenty tile-roofed casitas housing forty-three of the southland's most sumptuous rooms and suites. These privately situated units, with landscaped patios dotted with blue umbrellas, all have views of the valley.

Smallest—at more than one-thousand square feet, these are larger than some apartments—and least expensive among Rancho Valencia's accommodations are the twenty-five Del Mar rooms (from the high $200 range), each with a comfortable living area and wet bar. Sliding French doors open to a private terrace, and open-beamed ceilings make the rooms appear even larger.

Budget permitting, there are fifteen very large Rancho Santa Fe suites (from the upper $300 range) with similarly luxurious appointments. Be sure to ask about the resort's romance packages.

THE INN AT RANCHO SANTA FE
P.O. Box 869, Rancho Santa Fe, CA 92067
Telephone: (619) 756-1131; toll-free (800) 654-2928

Eighty rooms, each with private bath, telephone, and television; thirty-one have fireplaces; many have wet bars, kitchenettes, and/or private patios. Restaurant, swimming pool, English croquet course, small gym, and tennis courts on-site. Guest memberships available at two nearby golf courses. Beach cottage available to guests. Handicapped access. Moderate to deluxe.

GETTING THERE
From Interstate 5 (San Diego Freeway), take the Lomas Santa Fe Drive (S-8) exit. The inn is located approximately four miles east on this road. From Interstate 15, exit at the Valley Parkway exit at Escondido and drive eleven miles south on this route. The inn is approximately two to three hours from Los Angeles.

THE INN AT
RANCHO SANTA FE

Rancho Santa Fe

*F*ew Southern California inns have matured as gracefully as the Inn at Rancho Santa Fe. In operation for more than fifty years and family-operated since the 1950s, the inn owes much of its success to the steady guiding hand of the Royce family, which has run the property for three generations.

Boasting some twenty acres of lovingly tended grounds, the inn is a town landmark and a source of pride for the locals. Palms, magnolias, avocados, citrus trees, and acacias, as well as expanses of lush lawn, are nurtured by a small army of gardeners. The grounds are in constant bloom.

Also in abundance are towering eucalyptus trees, planted around the turn of the century by the Santa Fe Railroad as a source for railroad ties. The experiment failed when eucalyptus was found unsuitable for that purpose.

In an effort to recoup some of its investment, Santa Fe began selling residential lots and built an adobe guest house to accommodate prospective buyers. That tile-roofed structure now serves as the inn's main building.

Rooms for Romance

You won't find frilly canopies, coordinated wallpapers, or multilayered bed coverings here. The inn continues to decorate its guest rooms in a comfy, traditional style. The kitchenettes and glass-doored cupboards found in many rooms are especially reminiscent of the inn's early days, when famous guests like Douglas Fairbanks, Howard Hughes, Mary Pickford and Errol Flynn relaxed here.

Rooms are contained in a series of ranch-style cottage units carrying names like Juniper, Camellia, and Manzanita. For a romantic getaway, we suggest one of the larger bedrooms equipped with fireplace and patio (some also have kitchenettes) offered in the mid $150 range; the one- to three-bedroom private cottages run from around $300 to nearly $500 per night.

Appendix

MORE SOUTHERN CALIFORNIA ROMANTIC DESTINATIONS

After settling on our final listing of fifty romantic getaways in the south state, we discovered a few additional noteworthy inns and small hotels. They include:

Garden Street Inn
1212 Garden Street
San Luis Obispo, CA 93401
(805) 545-9802

The Inn/L'Auberge Del Mar
1540 Camino del Mar
Del Mar, CA 92014
(619) 259-1515; toll-free in
California (800) 553-1336

Hotel Metropole
On the waterfront in Avalon,
Catalina Island
P.O. Box 1900
Avalon, CA 90704
Toll-free (800) 541-8528

Saddleback Inn
Lake Arrowhead Village
P.O. Box 1890
Lake Arrowhead, CA 92352
(714) 336-3571

Ventana
Highway 1
Big Sur, CA 93920
(408) 667-2331

MORE TRAVEL RESOURCES FOR INCURABLE ROMANTICS

Weekends for Two in Northern California:
50 Romantic Getaways
With more than 150 color photos, this is the best-selling travel classic that started the "romantic revolution."
By Bill Gleeson and John Swain
Chronicle Books

For updates on future romantic getaway guidebooks in this series, write to Bill Gleeson in care of Chronicle Books, 275 Fifth Street, San Francisco, CA 94103.

Places of the Heart:
Romantic Inns of North America
P.O. Box 6324, Folsom, CA 95630
Romantic Inns of North America is an exclusive collection of the most romantic inns and small hotels in the United States and Canada. Write for a free guide which includes pictures and descriptions of each.

Index

C A S T   Y O U R   V O T E !

Southern California's Most Romantic Hotel or Inn

Complete and mail to Bill Gleeson, *Weekends for Two in Southern California*, Chronicle Books, 275 Fifth Street, San Francisco, California 94103. We'll return the favor by keeping you informed of our new romantic discoveries.

Our favorite Southern California romantic retreat:

_____

Name of hotel/inn:

_____

City/Town:

_____

What makes this place special:

_____

_____

_____

_____

Your name/address (if you wish to receive romantic updates; addresses/names are not for publication).